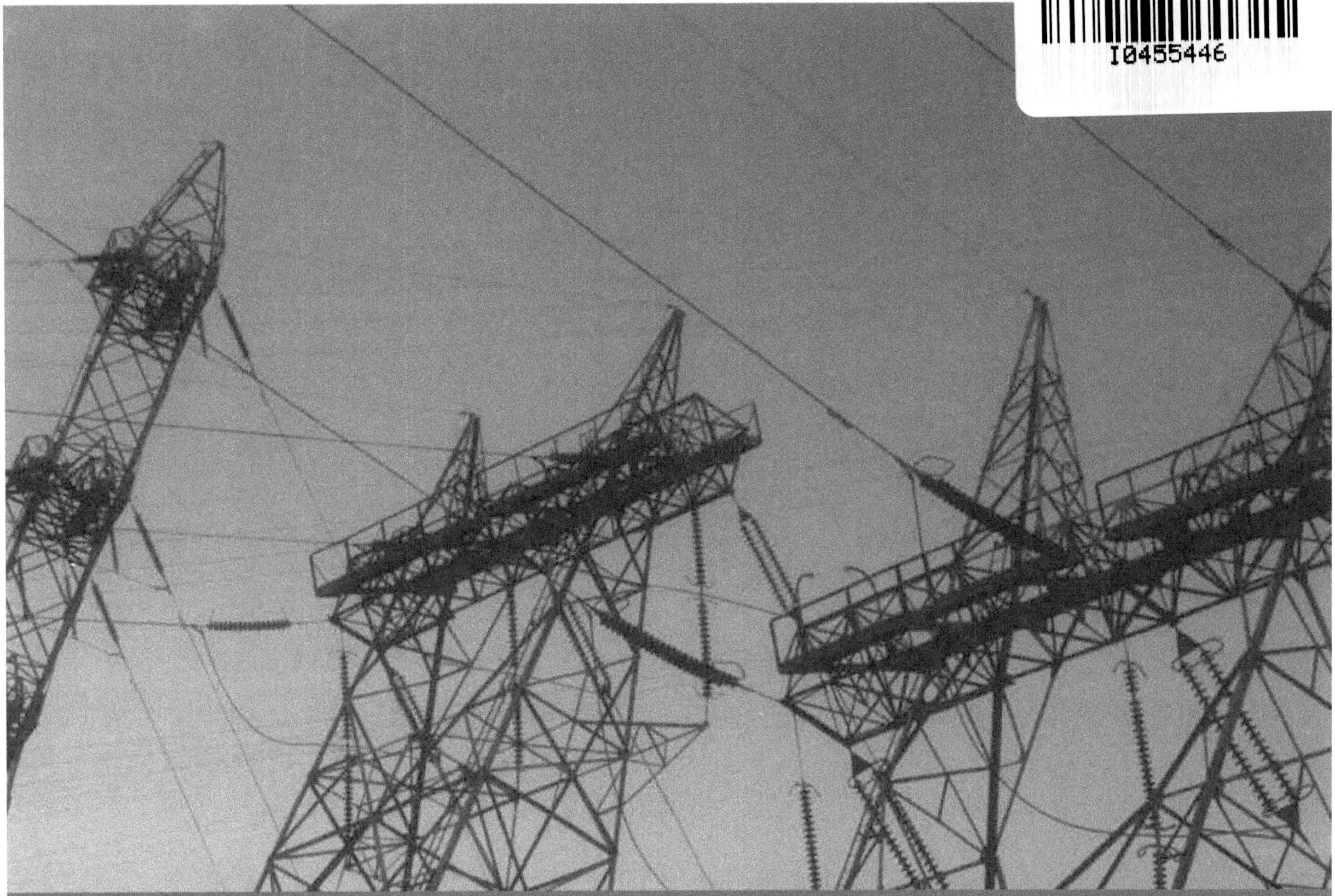

Energy
Sector-Specific Plan

An Annex to the National Infrastructure Protection Plan

2010

United States
Department
of Energy

Preface

In its role as the lead Sector-Specific Agency for the Energy Sector, the Department of Energy has worked closely with dozens of government and industry partners to prepare this updated 2010 Energy Sector-Specific Plan (SSP). Much of that work was conducted through the two Energy Sector Coordinating Councils (SCCs) and the Energy Government Coordinating Council (GCC). The Electricity SCC and the Oil and Natural Gas SCC comprise the Energy SCC and represent the interests of their respective industries. The Energy GCC represents all levels of government – Federal, State, local, territorial, and tribal – that are concerned with the Energy Sector.

We have received considerable support from our sector partners in this effort. The development process included joint writing teams, two formal rounds of reviews, and the consideration of hundreds of comments.

The Energy Sector has long prepared for all hazards, and natural disasters have been a key focus of sector efforts. The 2010 plan introduces several new topics including pandemic events and highlights cybersecurity activities. Protecting and improving the resilience of the Energy Sector in the face of both manmade and natural disasters will be an ongoing effort that will require continued vigilance, contingency planning, and training. The sector vision and goals communicate the physical and cyber preparedness, protective, and recovery measures that the government and infrastructure owners and operators are working together to achieve.

Perhaps the most valuable aspect of the SSP development process has been the ongoing development of a trusted relationship and true partnership between government and industry. This partnership has enabled the development of a unified vision for the sector, and it will continue to facilitate the national effort to implement the sector's critical infrastructure and key resources (CIKR) protective programs. Examples of Energy Sector accomplishments enabled by this partnership include:

- The North American Electric Reliability Corporation, acting as the federally authorized electric reliability organization, has developed several additional reliability standards for the power grid during the past year. These standards have been approved by the Federal Energy Regulatory Commission.

- Both the Electricity subsector and the Oil and Natural Gas subsector have initiated enhanced approaches to plan for and counter cybersecurity threats to energy infrastructure operations.

- In 2009, the Energy Sector worked very closely with the Chemical Sector to implement new rules regarding safety and security at chemicals facilities, many of which are also energy-related facilities and infrastructure.

- The Oil and Natural Gas SCC developed an Emergency Response Working Group and hosted several cross-sector emergency management workshops, which aim to promote an integrated private sector and government response during natural disasters and terrorist incidents.

- The sector established a working group under the Critical Infrastructure Partnership Advisory Council to develop sector-specific approaches to metrics in order to better track and report on sector advances.

- In the past year, the Energy Sector has made substantial progress in planning for impacts on operations from a pandemic. The appearance of the H1N1 virus has further heightened sector sensitivity to this issue.

This 2010 Energy SSP should not be considered complete. The Energy Sector is sure to face new challenges in the future, and new opportunities and pathways will develop over time. Several areas are certain to require further efforts, including: the resilience of supply chains, interdependencies between the Energy Sector and other sectors, analyzing the Energy Sector as a system, preparation for high impact but low probability events, development and implementation of meaningful metrics to assess sector progress, as well as the challenge of ensuring cybersecurity. The sector will also face continuing challenges from both natural and manmade events, both foreign and domestic.

Each year, the Energy Sector CIKR Protection Annual Report will provide updates on the sector's efforts to identify, prioritize, and coordinate the protection of its critical infrastructure. The Sector Annual Report provides the current priorities of the sector as well as the progress made during the past year in following the plans and strategies set out in the Energy SSP.

Through the partnership created under the NIPP framework, SCC and GCC partners will continue to work together to improve cooperation, with the ultimate end-goal of ensuring the protection and resilience of the American energy system.

Sincerely,

Patricia Hoffman

Assistant Secretary
Electricity Delivery and Energy Assurance
U.S. Department of Energy

Todd M. Keil

Assistant Secretary for Infrastructure Protection
U.S. Department of Homeland Security

Gerald W. Cauley

President and Chief Executive Officer
North American Electric
Reliability Corporation

Ron Jorgensen

2009 Chair, Oil and Natural Gas
Sector Coordinating Council
Questar Pipeline Company

Jay Montgomery

2010 Chair, Oil and Natural Gas
Sector Coordinating Council
Kinder Morgan

Table of Contents

List of Figures

List of Tables

Executive Summary

In January 2009, the U.S. Department of Homeland Security (DHS) announced completion of the revised version of the National Infrastructure Protection Plan (NIPP), a comprehensive risk management framework that defines critical infrastructure protection (CIP) roles and responsibilities for all levels of government, private industry, and other sector partners. The U.S. Department of Energy (DOE) has been designated the Sector-Specific Agency (SSA) for the Energy Sector,[1] and is tasked with coordinating preparation and implementation of an Energy Sector-Specific Plan (SSP) that is an annex to the NIPP.

In its role as Energy SSA, DOE has worked closely with dozens of government and industry partners to prepare this 2010 Energy SSP. Much of that work was conducted through the Energy Sector Coordinating Councils (SCC), as well as through the Energy Government Coordinating Council (GCC). The Energy SCC is comprised of the Electricity SCC and the Oil and Natural Gas SCC, which represent the interests of their respective industries. The GCC, co-chaired by DHS and DOE, represents all levels of government—Federal, State, local, tribal, and territorial—that are concerned with the Energy Sector.

The Energy Sector has developed a vision statement and six sector goals that are used as the framework for developing and implementing effective protective measures.

Vision Statement
The Department of Energy and its sector partners envision a robust, resilient energy infrastructure in which continuity of business and services is maintained through secure and reliable information sharing, effective risk management programs, coordinated response capabilities, and trusted relationships between public and private partners at all levels of industry and government.

Sector Goals
Information Sharing and Communication
Goal 1: Establish robust situational awareness within the sector through timely, reliable, and secure information exchange among trusted public and private sector partners.

---

[1] The Energy Sector, as delineated by Homeland Security Presidential Directive 7 (HSPD-7), includes the production, refining, storage, and distribution of oil, gas, and electric power, except for hydroelectric and commercial nuclear power facilities. The "Energy Sector" is not monolithic, and contains many interrelated industries that support the exploration, production, transportation, and delivery of fuels and electricity to the U.S. economy. While the Energy Sector is defined by HSPD-7, this SSP recognizes that efforts toward sector resilience against all hazards will be accomplished through a variety of government, industry, and joint partnership activities. This SSP distinguishes between the Electricity subsector and the Oil and Natural Gas subsector, although for ease of reading, the terms "subsector" and "sector" are used interchangeably when referring to these two Energy Sector segments.

Sector Goals
Physical and Cyber Security
Goal 2: Use sound risk management principles to implement physical and cyber measures that enhance preparedness, security, and resilience.
Coordination and Planning
Goal 3: Conduct comprehensive emergency, disaster, and continuity of business planning, including training and exercises, to enhance reliability and emergency response.
Goal 4: Clearly define critical infrastructure protection roles and responsibilities among all Federal, State, local, and private sector partners.
Goal 5: Understand key sector interdependencies and collaborate with other sectors to address them, and incorporate that knowledge in planning and operations.
Public Confidence
Goal 6: Strengthen partner and public confidence in the sector's ability to manage risk and implement effective security, reliability, and recovery efforts.

Energy Sector Profile and Assets

The Energy Sector, as defined by HSPD-7, consists of thousands of electricity, oil, and natural gas assets that are geographically dispersed and connected by systems and networks. Therefore, interdependency within the sector and across the Nation's critical infrastructure sectors is critical. The energy infrastructure provides fuel to the Nation, and in turn depends on the Nation's transportation, information technology, communications, finance, and government infrastructures. The energy systems and networks cross the Nation's borders, making international collaboration a necessary component of the sector's efforts to secure the energy infrastructure.

Protecting and improving the resilience of the Electricity and Oil and Natural Gas subsectors in the face of both manmade and natural disasters will be an ongoing effort that requires continued vigilance, contingency planning, and training. The combined sector vision and goals communicate the comprehensive physical and cyber preparedness, protective, and recovery measures that the government and infrastructure owners and operators are working together to achieve for the sector.

The sector already has substantial information sources in place to support critical infrastructure and key resources (CIKR)[2] protection, planning, and analysis. Collected by owners and operators, trade associations, and government organizations, this information identifies energy assets, systems, and networks. Any critical information that is voluntarily provided to DHS or DOE is expected to be protected by the Protected Critical Infrastructure Information (PCII) Program per the Critical Infrastructure Information Act of 2002 (CII Act). The CII Act provides that information submitted under the PCII Program is protected from public disclosure. In addition to the PCII Program, established communication channels among the sector partners will enable such critical information to be shared whenever necessary to facilitate protection and recovery of CIKR.

---

[2] CIKR can be defined as the assets, systems, and networks that provide vital services to the United States.

CIKR Assessment and Prioritization

Historically, DOE, other government agencies, and sector partners have been proactive in developing and applying vulnerability assessment methodologies. However, no single methodology is universally applicable. Because of the diversity of assets and systems in the sector, a multitude of methodologies is used to assess risks - threats, vulnerabilities, and consequences. The sector's threat analysis encompasses natural events, criminal acts, and insider threats, as well as foreign and domestic terrorism. Currently, a number of tools are being used to assess vulnerabilities, and the vast majority of significant facilities have already undergone assessments using one or more of the tools.

As the sector is characterized by very diverse assets and systems, prioritization of sector assets and systems is highly dependent upon changing threats and consequences. The significance of many individual components in the network is highly variable, depending on location, time of day, day of the week, and season of the year. Owners and operators of sector assets, whether oil and natural gas or electricity, have well-developed protocols in place to identify priorities and ensure business continuity and operational reliability. Therefore, prioritization of assets and systems in the sector needs to be flexible according to circumstances. Further dialogue among DOE, DHS, and other public and private stakeholders is necessary to examine cross-sector needs and approaches to support national infrastructure protection programs.

Protective Programs and Performance Measurement

With partnership as the cornerstone of its overall strategy, the sector already has more than 120 programs sponsored by dozens of public and private organizations that support its vision and goals. The programs fall within four main categories: 1) information sharing and communication, 2) physical and cyber security, 3) coordination and planning, and 4) public confidence. DOE, in conjunction with DHS, other government agencies, and private sector partners will continue to implement effective protective measures as it assesses the sector's CIKR protection needs, develops programs, and finds long-term solutions, including research and development (R&D).

Along with sector partners, DOE is in the process of developing an effective performance measurement system that identifies appropriate metrics for measuring progress, collects relevant data on each metric, and uses those data to improve performance and provide accountability. Energy sector-specific metrics will be developed by the sector partners. In addition, qualitative and quantitative measures to track progress toward the sector goals are currently being developed by the sector and will be periodically reviewed and modified as necessary. Almost all of the activities in the sector are already underway and will continue to be executed in coordination with all energy partners. Many examples of these activities and programs are detailed in the Energy Sector Annual Report, written yearly since 2006. Below are a few examples of successful activities:

- The SCC developed an Oil and Natural Gas SCC Emergency Response Working Group and hosted several cross-sector emergency management workshops, which aim to promote an integrated private sector and government response during natural disasters and terrorist incidents.

- The North American Electric Reliability Corporation, acting as the federally authorized electric reliability organization, has developed additional reliability standards for the power grid during the past year. These standards have been approved by the Federal Energy Regulatory Commission.

- In the past year, the Energy Sector has made substantial progress in planning for impacts on operations from a pandemic. The appearance of the H1N1 virus has further heightened sector sensitivity to this issue.

- The *Roadmap to Secure Control Systems in the Energy Sector*[3] (Control Systems Roadmap), which identifies concrete steps to secure control systems in the electricity, oil, and natural gas infrastructures through 2016. The Roadmap addressed the needs of the sector by establishing a vision and laying out a coherent plan for cybersecurity.

---

[3] www.oe.energy.gov/DocumentsandMedia/roadmap.pdf.

CIKR Protection R&D

Energy asset owners and operators have been working with government, national laboratories, universities, industry organizations, and other key stakeholders to drive technological innovation throughout the Electricity and Oil and Natural Gas subsectors. R&D includes infrastructure and cyber security. The 2006 *Roadmap to Secure Control Systems in the Energy Sector* established four main goals, and addresses the spectrum of cybersecurity priorities within the sector. The four goals are: 1) measure and assess security posture, 2) develop and integrate protective measures, 3) detect intrusion and implement response strategies, 4) and sustain security improvements. As improved infrastructure protection and resilience have become an increasingly significant objective of the sector's technology R&D, Federal R&D investments must be coordinated with the private sector to create an effective national R&D strategy for CIP.

Energy SSP Process and Responsibilities

DOE's Office of Electricity Delivery and Energy Reliability has been assigned the role and responsibilities of the Energy SSA, and will coordinate activities associated with the NIPP and Energy SSP. In doing so, DOE will maintain a close partnership with the Electricity and the Oil and Natural Gas SCCs and governmental partners through the Critical Infrastructure Protection Advisory Council (CIPAC). The Energy SSP will be updated on a regular basis, as the NIPP is updated. In addition to the Energy SSP, DOE, working with energy partners, will submit an annual CIKR report to DHS.

Perhaps the most valuable aspect of the SSP development process has been the ongoing growth of open communication, trusted relationships, and true partnership between government and industry. This partnership has enabled the development of a unified vision for sector protection and resilience, and it will continue to facilitate the national effort to implement the Electricity and Oil and Natural Gas subsectors' CIKR-protective programs.

Introduction

On June 30, 2006, the U.S. Department of Homeland Security (DHS) announced completion of the National Infrastructure Protection Plan (NIPP), a comprehensive risk management framework that defines critical infrastructure protection (CIP) roles and responsibilities for all levels of government, private industry, and other sector partners. The NIPP builds on the principles of the President's National Strategy for Homeland Security[4] and strategies for the protection of critical infrastructure and key resources (CIKR). The NIPP was reissued in January 2009.

The NIPP fulfills the requirements of the Homeland Security Act of 2002, which assigns DHS the responsibility to develop a comprehensive national plan for securing CIKR, as well as Homeland Security Presidential Directive 7 (HSPD-7), which provides overall guidance for developing and implementing the national CIP program. In accordance with HSPD-7, the national infrastructure is divided into 18 distinct CIKR sectors, and CIKR protection responsibilities are assigned to select Federal agencies called Sector-Specific Agencies (SSAs).

The U.S. Department of Energy (DOE) has been designated the Energy SSA. In this role, it has closely collaborated with dozens of government and industry partners to rewrite and revise the 2007 Energy Sector-Specific Plan (SSP). DOE also conducted formal review and comment periods for the draft 2010 Energy SSP.

CIKR protection and resilience are not new concepts to Energy Sector asset owners and operators. The Electricity and Oil and Natural Gas subsectors have faced challenges from both natural and man made events well before September 11, 2001. Since that time, the Energy Sector has made significant progress in developing plans to protect the energy CIKR and to prepare for restoration and recovery in response to terrorist attacks or natural disasters. More recently, potential threats from cyber penetration have created new concerns and industry responses. Through the Energy SSP process, government and industry have established unprecedented cooperation and close partnership to develop and implement a national effort that brings together all levels of government, industry, and international partners. This updated 2010 Energy SSP is a reflection of that partnership and the achievements of the sector over the last three years.

---

[4] The National Strategy for Homeland Security is the first national strategy established in the aftermath of the September 11, 2001 attacks. Released in July 2002, it is a comprehensive plan for using America's talents and resources to enhance CIKR protection and reduce vulnerability to terrorist attacks.

The Energy SSP is structured around the risk management framework defined in the NIPP:

Figure I-1: NIPP Risk Management Framework

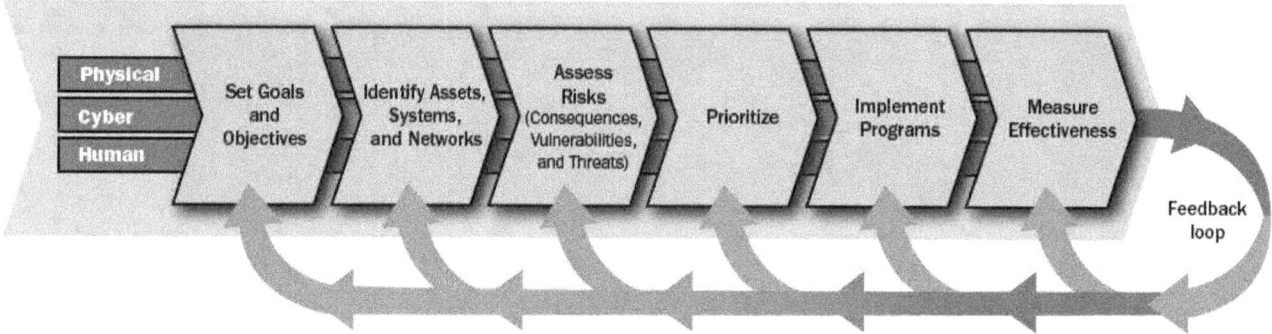

Continuous improvement to enhance protection of CIKR

1. Sector Profile, Vision, and Goals

Figure 1-1: Establishing Sector Goals

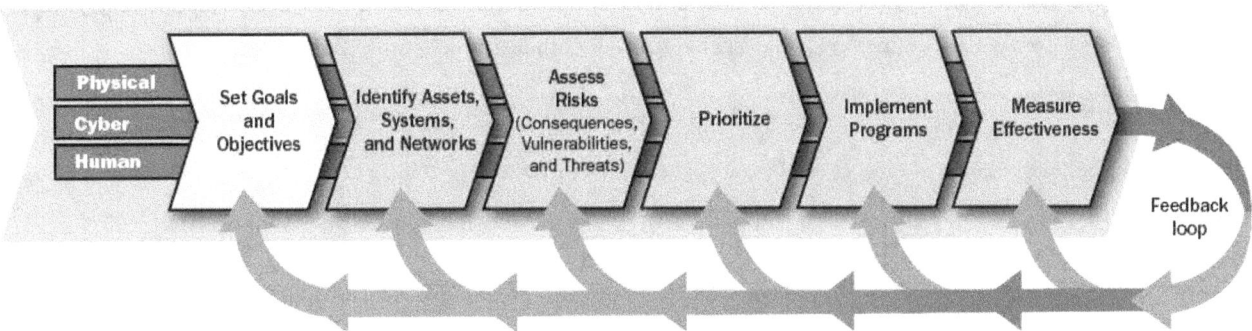

Continuous improvement to enhance protection of CIKR

A healthy energy infrastructure is one of the defining characteristics of a modern global economy. Any prolonged interruption of the supply of basic energy—electricity, petroleum, or natural gas—would do considerable harm to the U.S. economy and the American people.

Numerous characteristics of the Nation's energy infrastructure, including the wide diversity of owners and operators and the variety of energy supply alternatives and delivery mechanisms, make protecting it a challenge. Energy infrastructure assets and systems are geographically dispersed. Millions of miles of electricity lines and oil and natural gas pipelines and many other types of assets exist in all 50 States and Territories. In many cases these assets and systems are interdependent. In addition, the Energy Sector is subject to regulation in various forms.

DOE will continue to work with its Energy Sector partners to improve awareness and information sharing, implement measures to protect and enhance the resilience of physical and cyber assets, conduct emergency planning, clarify roles and responsibilities, understand and address interdependencies, and maintain public confidence. This chapter describes sector goals, the key characteristics of the electricity, oil, and natural gas industries; and the extensive public/private partnership involved in identifying security risks, protecting the energy infrastructure, and promoting sector resilience. Appendix 3 provides a brief summary of Federal legislative authorities related to the Energy Sector, and appendix 4 shows types of major asset ownership.

1.1 Sector Vision and Goals

Sector vision and goals communicate the comprehensive preparedness, protective, and resilience measures that the government and infrastructure owners and operators are working together to achieve. They are intended to reflect the sector's overall risk management focus and strategy, and to guide the activities of the NIPP risk management framework.

The Energy Sector used a collaborative process to develop its vision statement and sector goals. In its role as the designated SSA for energy, DOE collaborates with two Sector Coordinating Councils (SCCs)—one for electricity and one for oil and natural gas—and with a Government Coordinating Council (GCC) composed of members from all levels of government. These coordinating councils represent nearly all members of the energy community. They are committed not only to working closely with DOE, DHS, and other government Energy Sector partners, but also to work together to develop and refine the vision and goals for the sector and to achieve these goals in an efficient manner.

1.1.1 Vision Statement

The Energy Sector envisions a robust, resilient energy infrastructure in which continuity of business and services is maintained through secure and reliable information sharing, effective risk management programs, coordinated response capabilities, and trusted relationships between public and private partners at all levels of industry and government.

1.1.2 Goals

Information Sharing and Communication

- **Goal 1:** Establish robust situational awareness within the Energy Sector through timely, reliable, and secure information exchange among trusted public and private sector partners.

Physical and Cyber Security

- **Goal 2:** Use sound risk management principles to implement physical and cyber measures that enhance preparedness, security, and resilience.

Coordination and Planning

- **Goal 3:** Conduct comprehensive emergency, disaster, and continuity of business planning, including training and exercises, to enhance reliability and emergency response.

- **Goal 4:** Clearly define and clarify CIP roles and responsibilities among all Federal, State, local, and private sector partners, and work to create efficiency and improved coordination throughout the partnership.

- **Goal 5:** Understand key sector interdependencies and collaborate with other sectors to address them, and incorporate that knowledge in planning and operations.

Public Confidence

- **Goal 6:** Strengthen partner and public confidence in the sector's ability to manage risk and implement effective security, reliability, and recovery efforts.

1.2 Sector Profile

The Energy Sector includes assets related to three key energy resources: electric power, petroleum, and natural gas. Each of these resources requires a unique set of supporting activities and assets, as shown in table 1-1. Petroleum and natural gas share similarities in methods of extraction, fuel cycles, and transport, but the facilities and commodities are separately regulated and have multiple stakeholders and trade associations. The electric power industry is diverse in its ownership, geography, and asset type and is regulated by multiple levels of government.

Energy assets and critical infrastructure components are owned by private, Federal, State, and local entities, as well as by some types of energy consumers, such as large industries and financial institutions (often for backup power purposes). Types of major asset ownership are shown in appendix 4.

Table 1-1: Segments of the Energy Sector

Electricity	Petroleum	Natural Gas

• Generation
  – Fossil Fuel Power Plants
    » Coal
    » Natural Gas
    » Oil
  – Nuclear Power Plants[a]
  – Hydroelectric Dams[a]
  – Renewable Energy
• Transmission
  – Substations
  – Lines
  – Control Centers
• Distribution
  – Substations
  – Lines
  – Control Centers
• Control Systems
• Electricity Markets
	• Crude Oil
	  – Onshore Fields
	  – Offshore Fields
	  – Terminals
	  – Transport (pipelines)[a]
	  – Storage
	• Petroleum Processing Facilities
	  – Refineries
	  – Terminals
	  – Transport (pipelines)[a]
	  – Storage
	  – Control Systems
	  – Petroleum Markets
		• Production
		  – Onshore Fields
		  – Offshore Fields
		• Processing
		• Transport (pipelines)[a]
		• Distribution (pipelines)[a]
		• Storage[b]
		• Liquefied Natural Gas Facilities[b]
		• Control Systems
		• Gas Markets

[a] Hydroelectric dams, nuclear facilities, rail, and pipeline transportation are covered in other SSPs.

[b] Certain infrastructure of this asset type are regulated by the Chemical Facility Anti-Terrorism Standards (CFATS). The final tiering of the facilities covered by the CFATS was not completed at the time of this report.

1.2.1 Electricity

The electricity portion of the Energy Sector includes the generation, transmission, and distribution of electricity (figure 1-2). The use of electricity is ubiquitous, spanning all sectors of the U.S. economy. Electric power sector accounts for 40 percent of all energy consumed in the United States.[5] Although some significant regional differences exist, more than 98 percent of electricity is generated domestically, though some of the fuels used to generate electricity are imported.[6]

Figure 1-2: Overview of the Electric Power System and Control Communications

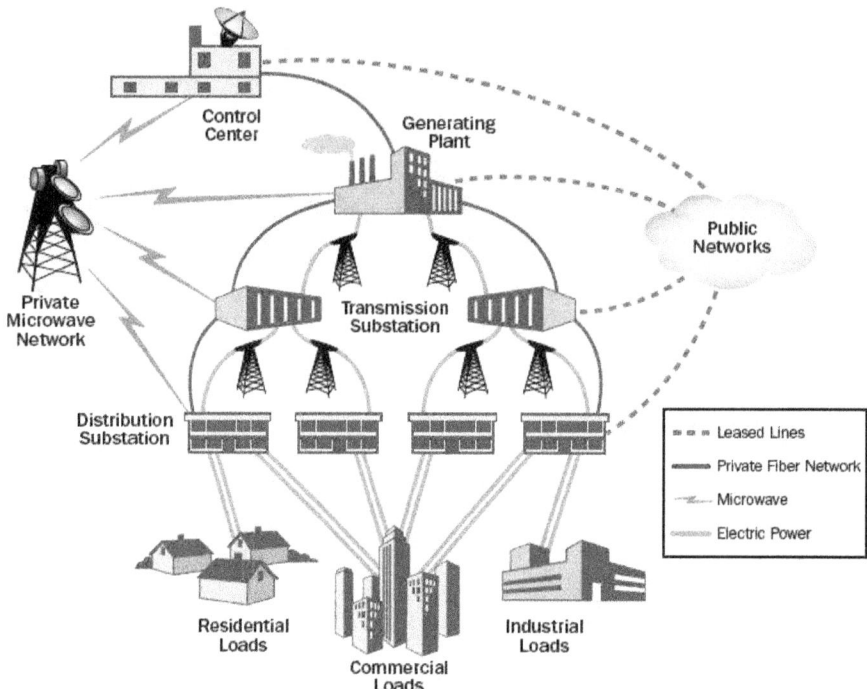

Electricity system facilities are dispersed throughout the North American continent.[7] Although most assets are privately owned, no single organization represents the interests of the entire sector. NERC,[8] through its eight Regional Reliability Councils, provides a platform for ensuring reliable, adequate, and secure supplies of electricity through coordination with the many asset owners.

1.2.1.1 Electricity Generation

The burning of fossil fuels (coal, natural gas, and oil) provides more than 70 percent of the total electricity generated in the U.S., as shown in figure 1-4. Virtually all coal is mined domestically and then transported to power plants by rail and barge. Natural gas and oil are transported to power plants by pipeline.

Several key sources of electricity generation are covered in other SSPs. The nuclear industry is regulated by the Nuclear Regulatory Commission (NRC), an independent Federal agency. Further discussion of nuclear power is provided in the Nuclear

---

[5] EIA, *Annual Energy Review* 2009, U.S. Primary Energy Consumption by Source and Sector, http://www.eia.doe.gov/emeu/aer/pecss_diagram.html (June 26, 2009).

[6] EIA, *Annual Energy Review* 2009, Table 8.1 Electricity Overview, http://www.eia.doe.gov/emeu/aer/txt/stb0801.xls (June 26, 2009).

[7] Important electric systems are also found in Alaska, Hawaii, and the U.S. Territories.

[8] NERC was founded as a nonprofit organization in 1968. It was designated as the Electric Reliability Organization (ERO) by the Federal Energy Regulatory Commission following passage of the Energy Policy Act of 2005. As a result of the law, NERC's official name changed to the North American Electric Reliability Corporation, effective January 1, 2007. The ERO will develop and enforce mandatory reliability standards for the bulk electric power system in the United States, Canada, and a portion of Baja Mexico.

Figure 1-3: 2008 Electric Infrastructure Data[a]

- 6,413 power plants[b]
- 3,273 traditional electric utilities[c]
- 1,738 nonutility power producers[d]

- 30,320 substations[e]
- 203,930 miles high-voltage AC transmission lines[f]

- 6,222 miles of high-voltage DC transmission lines[g]
- 143 million customers[h]

Note: Also see figure 1-5 for detailed breakdown of traditional electric utilities.

[a] Figure 1-3 represents 2008 data unless otherwise stated in the footnote. Note, however, that certain 2008 EIA electricity data were marked as preliminary at the time of this report.

[b] EIA, Form EIA-860 Database Annual Electric Generator Report, **http://www.eia.doe.gov/cneaf/electricity/page/eia860.html** (October 2009).

[c] 2007 data; EIA, "Composition of Electric Entities in the United States," **http://www.eia.doe.gov/cneaf/electricity/page/prim2/toc2.html**.

[d] Id.

[e] 2009 data; Energy Velocity (October 2009).

[f] NERC, Transmission Availability Data System (TADS) Working Group, NERC-2008-TADS TO TEMPLATE, **http://www.nerc.com/filez/tadswg.html** (July 14, 2009).

[g] Id.

[h] EIA, Electric Power Annual 2008, Table 7.1 Number of Ultimate Customers Served by Sector, by Provider, January 21, 2010, **http://www.eia.doe.gov/cneaf/electricity/epa/epaxlfile7_1.xls** (accessed July 27, 2010).

Reactors, Materials, and Waste SSP developed by DHS in partnership with NRC. In addition, the security of pipelines, which are critical for delivering oil and natural gas to power plants, is covered in the Pipeline Modal Annex to the Transportation Systems SSP (see appendix 7). Discussion of hydropower, including pumped storage, is provided in the Dams SSP developed by DHS in partnership with the U.S. Army Corps of Engineers (USACE), the Department of the Interior's (DOI) Bureau of Reclamation (BOR), and other public and private dam owners and operators.

Figure 1-4: 2008 U.S. Electric Power Capacity and Generation Profile[9]

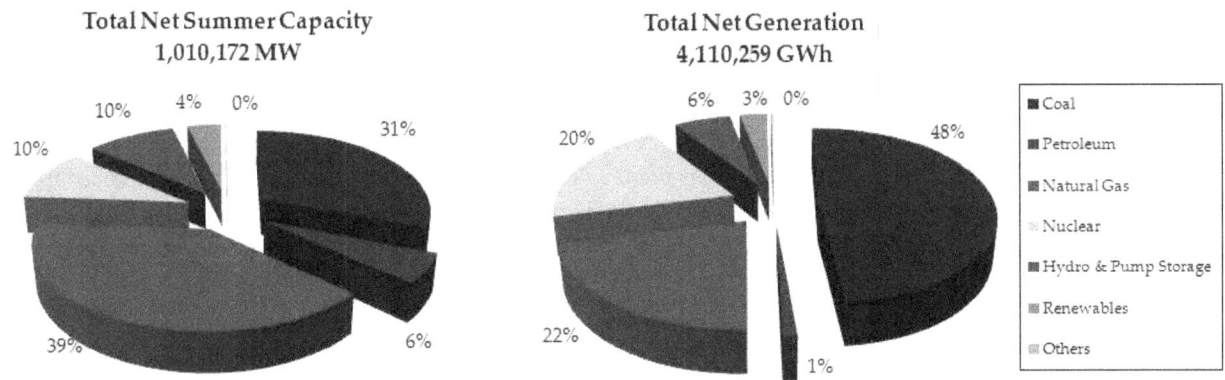

As shown in figure 1-4, in 2008 the United States had over 1,010 gigawatts (GW) of net summer capacity, 76 percent of which came from fossil fuel-fired power plants. Although natural gas-fired plants provided about 39 percent of the total net summer capacity, they produced only 22 percent of 4,110,259 gigawatt-hours (GWh) of total net generation in 2008. Coal remains the primary fuel source for electric power generation, accounting for almost half of the total net generation in the United States.

[9] EIA, *Annual Energy Review 2008*, Table 8.2a Electricity Net Generation: Total (All Sectors), June 26, 2009, **http://www.eia.doe.gov/aer/txt/stb0802a.xls** (accessed July 27, 2010); EIA, Table 8.11a Electric Net Summer Capacity: Total (All Sectors), January 21, 2010, **http://www.eia.doe.gov/aer/txt/stb0811a.xls** (accessed July 27, 2010).

In 2008, non-hydropower renewable energy sources (e.g., solar, wind, geothermal) accounted for 3 percent of total capacity and net generation. A growing percentage of national electricity generation is coming from various renewable sources, with the potential to provide alternative power sources for critical facilities and functions.

Figure 1-5: 2007 U.S. Traditional Electric Utilities by Ownership[10]

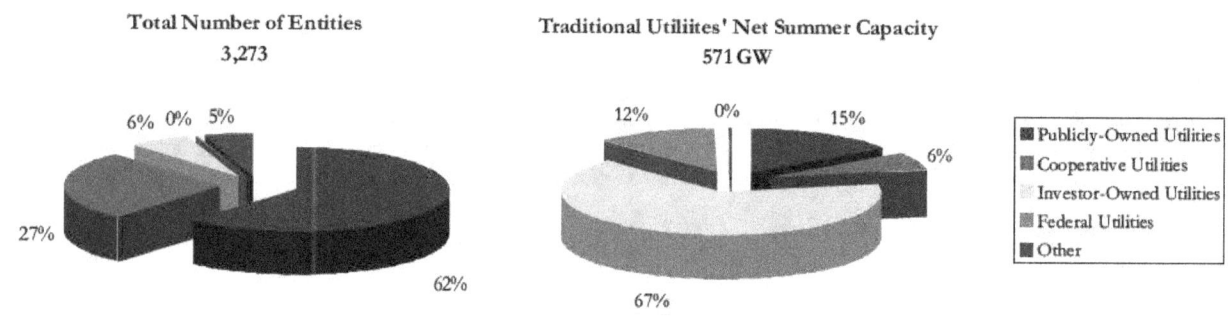

As of 2007, a total of 3,273 traditional electric utilities existed in the United States, providing 57 percent of the total net summer capacity (see figure 1-4 and figure 1-5). The rest, or 43 percent of the total capacity, came from 1,738 non-utility electric providers. Though small in number, investor-owned utilities (IOUs) accounted for 67 percent of the total net summer capacity of traditional electric utilities in the United States.

1.2.1.2 Electricity Transmission, Distribution, and Control Systems

Transmission lines. Transmission lines serve two primary purposes: They move electricity from generation sites to customers and they interconnect systems. Voltages in the transmission system are high, which makes it possible to carry electric power efficiently over long distances and deliver it to substations near customers.

Transmission and distribution substations. Substations are located at the ends of transmission lines. A transmission substation located near a power plant uses large transformers to increase the voltage. At the other end of a transmission line, a substation uses transformers to step transmission voltages back down so the electricity can be distributed to customers.

Control centers. Control centers have sophisticated monitoring and control systems and are staffed by operators 24 hours per day, 365 days per year. These operators are responsible for several key functions, including balancing power generation and demand, monitoring flows over transmission lines to avoid overloading, planning and configuring systems to operate reliably, maintaining system stability, preparing for emergencies, and placing equipment is and out of service for maintenance and during emergencies.

Distribution lines. Distribution lines carry electricity from substations to end users.

Control systems. Supervisory Control and Data Acquisition Systems (SCADA) and Distributed Control Systems (DCS) monitor the flow of electricity from generators through transmission and distribution lines. These electronic systems enable efficient operation and management of electric systems through the use of automated data collection and equipment control.

Smart Grid Technologies. Under the American Recovery and Reinvestment Act (ARRA) of 2009 funds have been made available to utilities to incorporate "smart technologies" into electricity distribution systems. These technologies are intended to improve end-use efficiency and increase the reliability of the grid.

[10] EIA, "Electric Power Industry Overview 2007," 2007, http://www.eia.doe.gov/cneaf/electricity/page/prim2/toc2.html (accessed July 27, 2010).

1.2.2 Petroleum

The petroleum portion of the Energy Sector includes the production, transportation, and storage of crude oil; processing of crude oil into petroleum products; transmission, distribution, and storage of petroleum products; and sophisticated control systems to coordinate storage and transportation (figures 1-6 to 1-8).

Petroleum supplied 37 percent of the total energy consumed in the United States in 2008.[11] Its primary use was in the transportation sector, which consumed 71 percent of the total petroleum supply. A total of 95 percent of the energy usage in the transportation sector came from petroleum.[12] Petroleum was used to lesser degrees in other sectors, accounting for 23 percent of energy used in the industrial sector, 5 percent in the residential and commercial sectors, and 1 percent in the electric power sector.[13]

As previously noted, pipelines, which are critical for the gathering, transmission, and distribution of petroleum and natural gas, are part of the Transportation Sector, and oversight of pipeline security is the responsibility of DHS' Transportation Security Administration (TSA). Pipeline security is specifically addressed in the Pipeline Modal Annex to the Transportation Systems SSP developed by TSA. The executive summary of the plan is also appended to the Energy SSP as appendix 7.

The Energy SSP does not address the chemical industry or the overlaps between the petrochemical industry and the transportation, storage, and processing of crude oil and refined petroleum products. Petrochemical facilities are addressed in the Chemical SSP. However, the Energy Sector collaborates with the Chemical Sector in the development of cross-sector metrics and the implementation of CFATS, among other activities.[14]

Figure 1-6: 2008 Petroleum Infrastructure Statistics[a]

Production[b]	525,000 producing wells
Processing[c]	150 petroleum refineries
Storage	1,400 petroleum terminals
Transportation[d]	835.4 billion ton miles
Pipeline Movements[e]	
Petroleum products	13.3 billion barrels per year
Annual Mileage of Pipeline Systems[f]	
Crude oil	46,571 annual miles onshore 5,001 annual miles offshore
Petroleum products	61,014 annual miles onshore 23 annual miles offshore

Note: Also see figure 1-7 for percent share by transportation mode in billion ton miles.

[a] Figure 1-6 represents 2008 data unless otherwise noted in the footnote. Note, however, that certain 2008 EIA electricity data are marked as preliminary at the time of this report.

[b] EIA, *Annual Energy Review 2009*, Table 5.2 Crude Oil Production and Crude Oil Well Productivity, **http://www.eia.doe.gov/emeu/aer/txt/stb0502.xls** (June 26, 2009).

[c] EIA, *Annual Energy Review 2009*, Table 5.9 Refinery Capacity and U tilization, **http://www.eia.doe.gov/emeu/aer/txt/stb0509.xls** (June 26, 2009).

[d] 2007 data, Association of Oil Pipe Lines, *2007 Report on Shifts in Petroleum Transportation*, **http://www.aopl.org/pdf/Shift_Report_Posted_September_2_20091.pdf** (September 2, 2009).

[e] **http://www.aopl.org/aboutPipelines/**.

[f] Department of Transportation's (DOT) Pipeline and Hazardous Material Safety Administration (PHMSA), Natural Gas Transmission, Gas Distribution, and Hazardous Liquid Pipeline Annual Mileage, **http://www.phmsa.dot.gov/pipeline/library/data-stats** (September 14, 2009).

Figure 1-7: 2007 Crude Oil and Products Transportation by Mode[f]

Total: 835.4 Billions of Ton miles

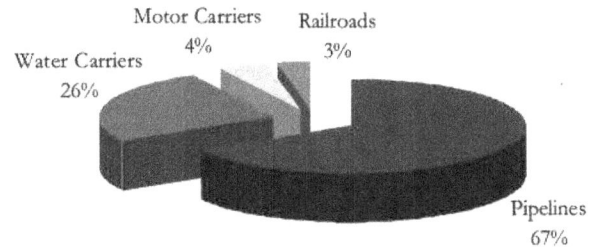

Motor Carriers 4%
Railroads 3%
Water Carriers 26%
Pipelines 67%

---

[11] EIA, *Annual Energy Review* 2009, U.S. Primary Energy Consumption by Source and Sector, http://www.eia.doe.gov/emeu/aer/pecss_diagram.html (June 26, 2009).

[12] EIA, *Annual Energy Review* 2009, U.S. Primary Energy Consumption by Source and Sector, http://www.eia.doe.gov/emeu/aer/pdf/pages/sec2_10.pdf.

[13] EIA, *Annual Energy Review* 2009, U.S. Primary Energy Consumption by Source and Sector, http://www.eia.doe.gov/emeu/aer/pdf/pages/sec2_6.pdf.

[14] DHS' Infrastructure Security Compliance Division (ISCD) leads the national implementation of CFATS. At the time of this report, there existed no defining roles or regulatory scheme specific to the Oil and Natural Gas SCC in regards to the ISCD's implementation of CFATS.

Figure 1-8: Overview of the Petroleum System

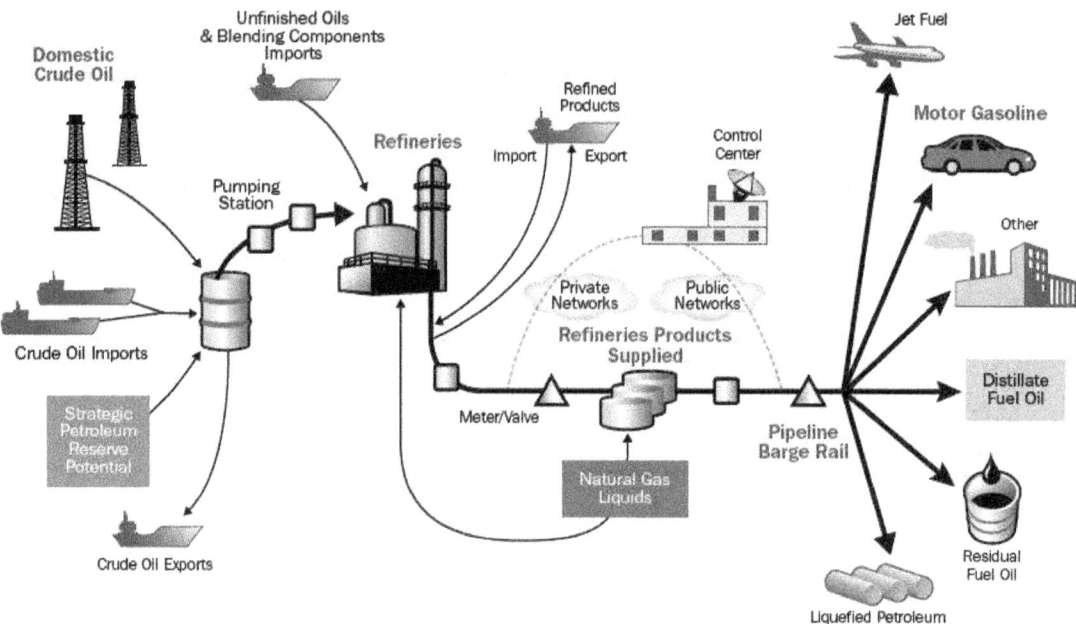

1.2.2.1 Crude Oil

Onshore and offshore fields. U.S. crude oil production is concentrated onshore and offshore along the Texas-Louisiana gulf coast, extending inland through western Texas, Oklahoma, and eastern Kansas. There are also significant oil fields in Alaska along the central North Slope. U.S. proven[15] crude oil reserves totaled an estimated 19.1 billion barrels at the close of 2008. More than three-quarters (80 percent) of U.S. reserves are in Alaska, California, Texas, and offshore areas. Petroleum production on the Alaskan North Slope is now equaled by output from the offshore areas in the Federal domain seaward of the California coastline and the western and central coasts of the Gulf of Mexico.

Crude oil drilling, gathering, and processing. The upstream sector of the petroleum industry includes a large number of facilities, such as wellheads, gas and oil separation plants, oil/gas dehydration units, emulsion breaker units, oil/gas sweetening units, compressor stations, water treatment units, etc., for both onshore and offshore areas.

Import marine terminals. U.S. dependence on foreign crude oil has grown from 15 percent in 1971 to 66 percent in 2008.[16] Crude oil is received into the United States at import terminals, which usually consist of berths or port facilities for tankers, unloading facilities, storage facilities, and a system of pipelines to move the crude.

Table 1-2: 2008 U.S. Oil Import Dependence[a]

U.S. Production	5.0 million barrels/day crude 1.8 million barrels/day natural gas plant liquids
Net Imports	9.8 million barrels/day crude 3.1 million barrels/day petroleum products
Import Dependence	66 percent of total crude oil supply

[a] EIA, *Annual Energy Review 2009*, tables 5.1, 5.3, and 5.5, June 2009, **http://www.eia.doe.gov/aer/pdf/aer.pdf** (accessed July 27, 2010).

---

[15] Reserves believed to be recoverable from known reservoirs under existing economic and operating conditions.

[16] EIA, *Annual Energy Review 2009*, Table 5.1 Petroleum Overview and 5.3 Petroleum Imports by Type, June 29, 2009, **http://www.eia.doe.gov/aer/pdf/aer.pdf** (accessed July 27, 2010).

Crude oil transport. Privately owned pipelines transport most of the crude oil in the United States. Waterborne transportation modes, including ocean tankers and barges, are also used. The United States imports more crude oil from Canada[17] than any other country, the majority of which enters the U.S. through pipelines.

Crude oil storage. Import terminals always incorporate storage facilities. At the end of 2008, U.S. crude oil inventories, including the Strategic Petroleum Reserve (SPR), totaled 702 million barrels.[18] More than two-thirds is stored in huge underground salt caverns at the SPR along the coastline of the Gulf of Mexico. The reserve has the capacity to hold 727 million barrels and is the world's largest supply of emergency crude oil.[19]

1.2.2.2 Petroleum Processing, Product Transport, and Storage

Refineries. Refineries process crude oil into petroleum products such as gasoline, diesel fuel, jet fuel, and home heating oil. The Gulf Coast has more than twice the crude oil distillation capacity of any other U.S. region. The number of U.S. oil refineries has declined from 213 in 1988 to 150 in 2008, while total capacity has increased by more than 1.7 million barrels per day (11 percent) to more than 17.6 million barrels per day.[20] Over the last five years, gross inputs to the Nation's refineries have been at their highest level in history, at nearly 15.5 million barrels per day—22 percent higher than the 5-year average for 1984-1988.[21] During the same time period, refineries have been operating at roughly 89 percent of capacity, with summer peak utilization rates of approximately 95 to 97 percent.

Petroleum product transport. Petroleum products are mainly transported by pipeline, tanker, or barge, but railroad tank cars or trucks are also used. The products are shipped to terminals for temporary storage before transport to smaller bulk plants in market areas.

Petroleum product storage. Petroleum products are stored both above and below ground in tank farms and storage fields to minimize unwanted fluctuations in pipeline throughput and product delivery. DOE's Northeast Home Heating Oil Reserve stores 2 million barrels of home heating oil at commercial terminals in the Northeast. This oil is intended for distribution during severe heating-oil supply disruptions in that part of the country.

1.2.2.3 Petroleum Control Systems

Control systems continuously monitor, transmit, and process pipeline data (e.g., flow rate, pressure, speed). SCADA systems monitor and control pumping stations and track terminal inventories.

1.2.3 Natural Gas

The natural gas portion of the Energy Sector includes the production, processing, transportation, distribution, and storage of natural gas; liquefied natural gas (LNG) facilities; and gas control systems (figures 1-9 and 1-10).

Natural gas provided 24 percent of U.S. energy needs in 2008, and its use is growing.[22] In particular, power producers and industrial facilities are opting for gas-powered equipment, and residential customers use natural gas for heating and cooking.

---

[17] EIA, U.S. Imports by Country of Origin, June 29, 2010, **http://tonto.eia.doe.gov/dnav/pet/pet_move_impcus_a2_nus_ep00_im0_mbbl_m.htm** (accessed July 27, 2010).

[18] EIA, *Annual Energy Review 2009,* Table 5.17 Strategic Petroleum Reserve, **http://www.eia.doe.gov/emeu/aer/txt/stb0517.xls** (June 26, 2009). In an energy emergency, SPR oil would be distributed by competitive sale. Decisions to withdraw crude oil from the reserve are made by the President under the authorities of the Energy Policy and Conservation Act (42 U.S.C. 6241(d)(1).

[19] DOE, Office of Fossil Energy, **www.fe.doe.gov/programs/reserves/spr/spr-facts.html**.

[20] EIA, *Annual Energy Review 2009,* Table 5.9 Refinery Capacity and Utilization, **http://www.eia.doe.gov/emeu/aer/txt/stb0509.xls** (June 26, 2009).

[21] EIA U.S. Gross Inputs to Refineries **http://tonto.eia.doe.gov/dnav/pet/hist/LeafHandler.ashx?n=PET&s=mgirius2&f=a**.

[22] EIA, *Annual Energy Review 2009,* U.S. Primary Energy Consumption by Source and Sector, **http://www.eia.doe.gov/emeu/aer/pecss_diagram.html** (June 26, 2009).

Although most of the natural gas consumed in the United States is produced domestically, imports have increased from 7.5 percent of total consumption in 1990 to 12.7 percent in 2008.[23]

1.2.3.1 Natural Gas Production, Processing, Transport, Distribution, and Storage

Natural gas production. Federal Offshore Gulf of Mexico and Texas are the largest gas-producing regions in the United States, at approximately 6.4 billion and 17.9 billion cubic feet per day, respectively.[24] The two regions account for almost 45 percent of all U.S. natural gas production. The United States had 245 trillion cubic feet of dry natural gas reserves as of December 31, 2008.[25]

Natural gas processing. Natural gas processing consists of separating all the various hydrocarbons and fluids from pure natural gas to produce pipeline-quality dry natural gas. Most U.S. natural gas processing plants are located near production facilities in the Southwest and Rocky Mountain States. The natural gas extracted from a well is transported to a processing plant through a network of gathering pipelines.

Natural gas transportation. The interstate natural gas pipeline network transports natural gas from processing plants in producing regions to market areas with high natural gas requirements, particularly large urban areas. Compression stations along the pipeline transmission route keep the gas moving at the desired volume and pressures.

Natural gas distribution. Local distribution companies typically transport natural gas from interstate pipeline delivery points to end users through millions of miles of distribution pipe. Delivery points to local distribution companies are often termed city gates, especially for large municipal areas, and are important market centers for the pricing of natural gas.

Natural gas storage. Gas is typically stored underground and under pressure as an efficient way to balance variations between supply input and market demand. Three types of

Figure 1-9: 2008 Natural Gas Infrastructure Statistics[a]

Production[b]	478,562 gas and condensate wells
Processing[c]	More than 500 gas processing plants (lower 48)
Storage[d]	401 underground storage facilities 8.5 trillion cubic feet capacity 109 LNG storage facilities
Pipeline[e]	
Gathering	20,215 miles of gathering pipeline
Transmission	298,993 miles of interstate pipeline
Distribution	1.2 million miles of intrastate pipeline

Sources: Production, processing, and storage data from EIA; gathering, transmission, and distribution from Pipeline and Hazardous Material Safety Administration's Pipeline Safety Program.

[a] Figure 1-9 represents 2008 data unless otherwise specified in the footnote.

[b] EIA, Natural Gas Number of Producing Gas Wells, June 29, 2010, http://tonto.eia.doe.gov/dnav/ng/ng_prod_wells_s1_a.htm (accessed July 27, 2010).

[c] EIA Report http://www.eia.doe.gov/pub/oil_gas/natural_gas/feature_articles/2006/ngprocess/ngprocess.pdf

[d] EIA, Natural Gas Underground Natural Gas Storage Capacity, June 29, 2010, http://www.eia.doe.gov/dnav/ng/ng_stor_cap_dcu_nus_a.htm (accessed July 27, 2010).

[e] The Department of Transportation's (DOT) Pipeline and Hazardous Material Safety Administration (PHMSA), Natural Gas Transmission, Gas Distribution, and Hazardous Liquid Pipeline Annual Mileage, http://www.phmsa.dot.gov/pipeline/library/data-stats (September 14, 2009).

Table 1-3: 2008 U.S. Natural Gas Import Dependence[a]

U.S. Production	21.3 trillion cubic feet
Net Imports	3.6 trillion cubic feet pipeline gas 0.35 trillion cubic feet LNG
Import Dependence	12.7 percent of total consumption

[a] EIA, Annual Energy Review 2009, Table 6.3 Natural Gas Import, Exports, and Net Imports, http://www.eia.doe.gov/emeu/aer/txt/stb0603.xls (June 26, 2009).

---

[23] EIA, Annual Energy Review 2009, Table 6.3 Natural Gas Imports, Exports, and Net Imports, http://www.eia.doe.gov/emeu/aer/txt/stb0603.xls (June 26, 2009).

[24] EIA, Natural Gas Gross Withdrawals and Production, June 29, 2010, http://tonto.eia.doe.gov/dnav/ng/ng_prod_sum_a_EPG0_FPD_mmcf_a.htm (accessed July 27, 2010).

[25] EIA, Natural Gas Reserves Summary, http://tonto.eia.doe.gov/dnav/ng/ng_enr_sum_dcu_NUS_a.htm (February 10, 2009).

Figure 1-10: Flow of Natural Gas

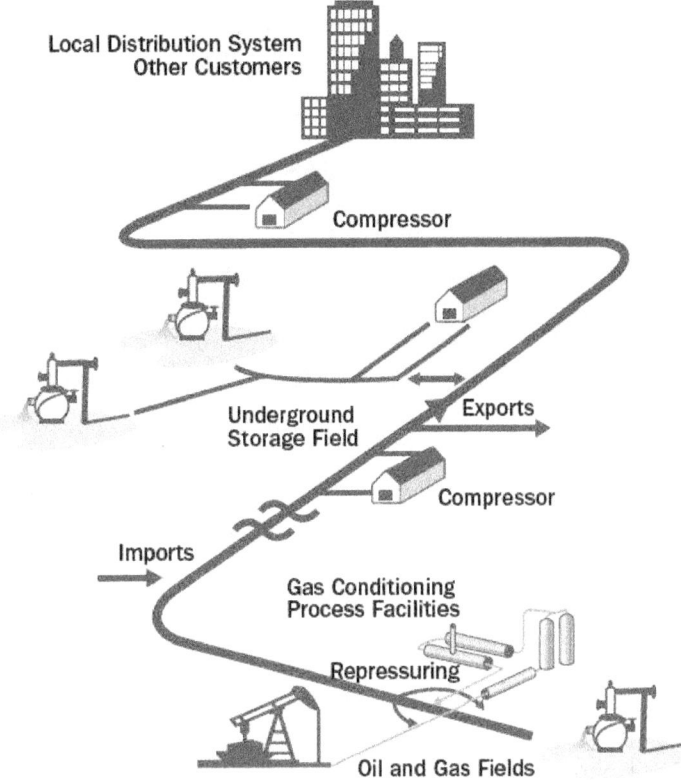

facilities are used for underground gas storage: depleted reservoirs in oil and/or gas fields, aquifers, and salt caverns. Facilities serving the interstate market are subject to Federal Energy Regulatory Commission (FERC) regulations; otherwise they are State-regulated. Most working gas held in storage facilities is held under lease with shippers, local distribution companies, or end users who own the gas.

1.2.3.2 Liquefied Natural Gas Facilities

LNG is produced by cooling natural gas to −260 degrees Fahrenheit (−160 degrees Centigrade). In its liquid state, natural gas occupies 618 times less volume than the same mass of gaseous methane at standard conditions, which allows it to be transported by specially designed ships or tankers. The lower 48 States have five marine terminals for receiving, storing, and regasifying LNG for delivery into the pipeline network, and more than 50 above-ground LNG storage tanks for meeting peak-day demand.[26] In addition, there is an LNG export terminal in Kenai, Alaska and another LNG import facility in Peñuelas, Puerto Rico.[27]

---

[26] FERC, http://www.ferc.gov/industries/lng/indus-act/terminals/exist-term.asp (April 17, 2009).
[27] Id.

1.2.3.3 Natural Gas Control Systems

To monitor and control the flow of natural gas, centralized gas control stations collect, assimilate, and manage data received from compressor stations all along the pipeline. These control systems can integrate gas flow and measurement data with other accounting, billing, and contract systems.

1.2.3.4 Gas Market Centers

Currently, a total of 33 natural gas market centers operate in the United States and Canada, 24 and nine, respectively.[28] These centers provide gas shippers with many of the physical capabilities and administrative support services formerly handled by interstate pipeline companies as bundled sales services (e.g., physical coverage of short-term receipt/delivery balancing needs). These centers have developed new and unique Internet-based access to gas trading platforms and capacity release programs; provide title transfer services between parties that buy, sell, or move gas through the centers; and offer connections with other pipelines and access to storage services. These markets centers and their information systems are important components of the natural gas infrastructure.

1.2.4 Energy Sector Interdependencies

Sector interdependencies. During the last half of the 20th century, technical innovations and developments in digital information and telecommunications dramatically increased interdependencies among the Nation's critical infrastructures. As shown in figure 1-11, each infrastructure depends on other infrastructures to function successfully. Disruptions in a single infrastructure can generate disturbances within other infrastructures and over long distances, and the pattern of interconnections can extend or amplify the effects of a disruption. The energy infrastructure provides essential fuel to all of the other critical infrastructures, and in turn depends on the Nation's transportation, information technology (IT), communications, finance, and government infrastructures. Over time cyber/IT dependencies have increased. For example, electricity and natural gas suppliers rely heavily on data collection systems to ensure accurate billing. Energy control systems and the information and communications technologies on which they rely play a key role in the North American energy infrastructure. They are essential in monitoring and controlling the production and distribution of energy. They have helped to create the highly reliable and flexible energy infrastructure in the United States.

Figure 1-11: Interdependencies Across the Economy

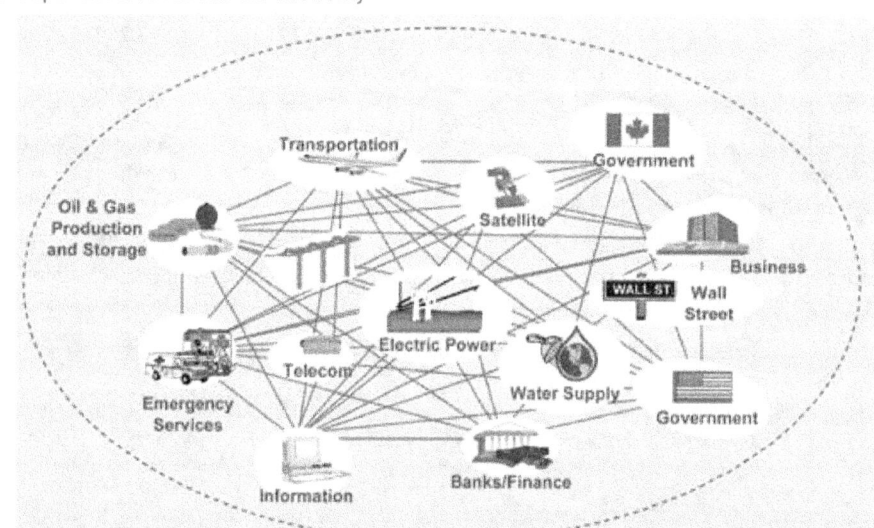

---

[28] EIA, Natural Gas Market Centers: A 2008 Update, **http://www.eia.doe.gov/pub/oil_gas/natural_gas/feature_articles/2009/ngmarketcenter/ngmarketcenter.pdf** (April 2009).

International interdependencies. Energy infrastructure interdependencies also cross international borders. Oil and natural gas pipelines and electric transmission lines have helped integrate the energy systems of North America. Moreover, increasing imports of petroleum products continue to highlight U.S. dependence on foreign oil. The United States also relies on imports of critical technologies, such as large-sized transformers.

1.2.5 Energy Sector Resilience

Energy infrastructure resilience is defined as the ability to reduce the magnitude and/or duration of disruptive events. The resilience of an infrastructure or enterprise depends on its ability to anticipate, absorb, adapt to, and/or rapidly recover from a disruptive event. Note that risk-based protective programs and resilience are complementary elements of the comprehensive risk management strategy pursued under the Energy SSP.

1.3 CIKR Partners

No single government agency, industry group, or company can secure the entire energy infrastructure. Collaboration at all levels is essential to securing an interdependent infrastructure that is owned, operated, hosted, and regulated by many entities. Voluntary partnerships help facilitate the useful exchange of security-related information and maximize the effectiveness of infrastructure protection and resilience efforts. They also promote the cooperation necessary to speed restoration and recovery with activities such as equipment and personnel sharing. DOE is working to coordinate critical energy infrastructure protection and resilience efforts with private, government, and international partners. The Energy SSP provides the basis for close and effective coordination among all sector partners.

1.3.1 Relationships With Industry Owners/Operators and Organizations

Figure 1-12 below depicts the current organizational structure of the Energy Sector partnership under the NIPP framework, including numerous working groups (WGs) that are managed by industry partners through the SCCs.

Figure 1-12: Energy Sector Public & Private Sector Working Groups

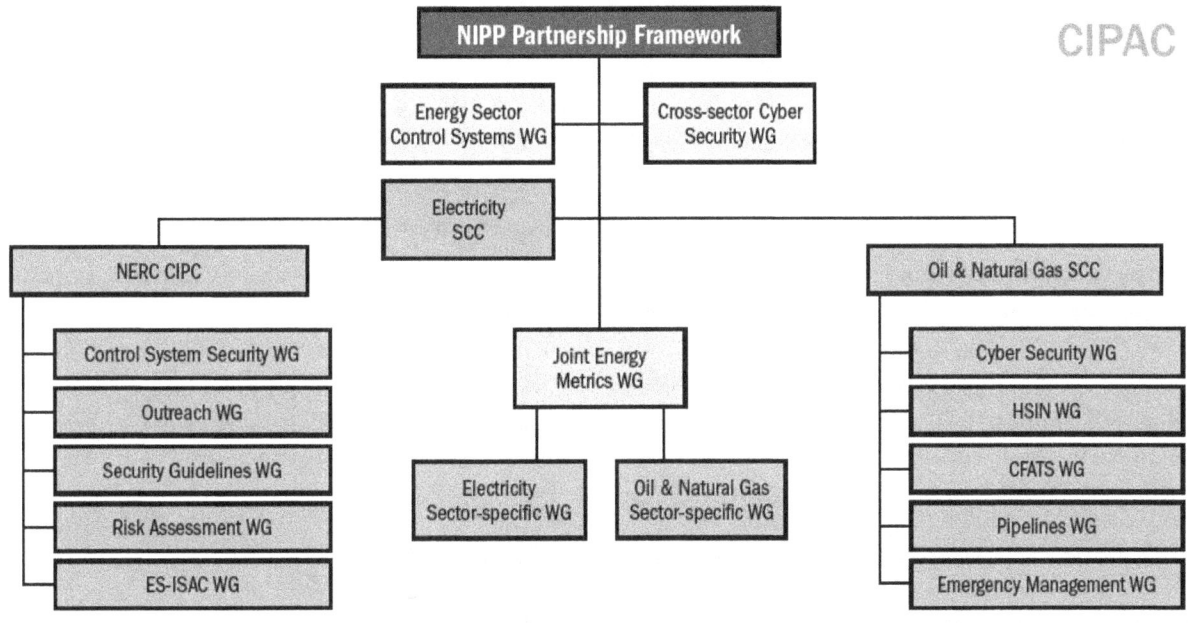

As defined in the NIPP, SCCs are created by owners and operators and are self-organized, self-run, and self-governed, with a leadership designated by the sector membership. SCCs serve as the principal body for coordinating with the Federal Government on a wide range of CIKR protection activities and issues.[29]

The Energy Sector established two SCCs in 2004 to coordinate industry initiatives under the public-private partnerships. The Electricity SCC (ESCC) represents the interests of electricity industry owners and operators and includes representatives from more than 30 industry organizations. It also includes the executive committee of NERC's Critical Infrastructure Protection Committee (CIPC), along with the president and chief executive officer of NERC.[30] The Oil and Natural Gas SCC (ONG SCC) represents the interests of ONG sector owners and operators with representatives from some 23 industry trade organizations. The council chairperson acts as the prime contact for DOE and DHS. The members of the ONG SCC also work on transportation sector pipeline efforts through the Pipeline Working Group that serves as the Pipeline Modal SCC for the Transportation Systems Sector.

As the Energy SSA, DOE works at many levels with the electricity, petroleum, and natural gas industries. It interacts with numerous trade associations and industry groups to share information, discuss coordination mechanisms, and promote scientific and technological innovation to support energy security.

1.3.2 Relationships With Government Agencies

1.3.2.1 Government Coordinating Council

The government counterpart for the SCCs is the Energy Sector GCC, which was also established in early 2004. The GCC is cochaired by DOE and DHS, and is composed of representatives across various levels of government (Federal, State, local, tribal, and territorial) that are concerned with the security of the Energy Sector.[31] The members of the Energy Sector GCC also work on pipeline efforts.

The Energy Sector GCC plays a critical role in the implementation of the Energy SSP. Through the partnership model, it maximizes efficiency by collaborating with sector partners at various levels and sectors. Together with Energy SCCs, the GCC works to develop and prioritize various security programs and initiatives supporting the NIPP and the Energy SSP.

1.3.2.2 Relationships With Other Federal Departments and Agencies

DOE has longstanding relationships with many Federal agencies to help fulfill its mission to provide safe and secure energy supplies. Several of these agencies have responsibilities critical to supporting the Energy Sector (see appendix 4, which provides a brief summary of Federal legislative authorities related to the Energy Sector). For example:

- **Department of Agriculture (USDA)**. USDA's Rural Utilities Service provides funding and support for rural electric utilities.

- **Department of Defense (DoD)**. The USACE maintains the Nation's dams, many of which are used for hydroelectric power. The USACE also maintains shipping channels ensuring transportation of petroleum and other products.

- **Department of Homeland Security (DHS)**. DHS, in coordination with DOE (as SSA for the Energy Sector), leads, integrates, and coordinates CIP activities across the Federal Government. As previously noted, certain segments of the Energy Sector are directly coordinated by DHS, including nuclear power and hydroelectric power (dams). DHS' Transportation Security Administration oversees pipeline security and works closely with the Department of Transportation (DOT) and DOE on

---

[29] DHS, 2009 *National Infrastructure Protection Plan*, section 4.1.2.3, p. 52, **http://www.dhs.gov/xlibrary/assets/NIPP_Plan.pdf** (March 2009).

[30] NERC, Critical Infrastructure Protection Committee, **http://www.nerc.com/page.php?cid=1|9|117|139** (accessed October 6, 2009).

[31] DHS, 2009 *National Infrastructure Protection Plan*, section 4.1.2.3, p. 52 **http://www.dhs.gov/xlibrary/assets/NIPP_Plan.pdf** (March 2009).

Figure 1-13: Emergency Management Working Group (EMWG)

Catastrophic events of the recent decade, including the terrorist attacks of September 11, 2001 and the gulf coast hurricanes of 2005 have emphasized the need for optimal emergency management (EM).[21] Many of the national plans and strategies that have emerged from those events have in fact increased the need for a better understanding of the disciplines involved in EM. To address these needs, the Oil and Natural Gas SCC, together with the Chemical SCC, has formed a joint Emergency Management Working Group (EMWG). Co-chaired by BP America and Valero Energy Corporation, the group strives to promote EM in the oil, natural gas, and chemical industries by facilitating discussion and sharing information. The EMWG's objectives are to:

- Increase communication with DOE, DHS, and other agencies in the Energy GCC and Chemical GCC with regard to managing incidents and emergencies;

- Promote EM as it pertains to infrastructure protection, and serve as a focal point on EM for national plans and programs;

- Provide a forum for industry and government agencies to share information on Federal regulations and programs that could affect EM activities and programs;

- Facilitate dialogues between industry members to help individual companies develop and assess EM;

- Discuss EM practices and lessons learned, and;

- Serve as a liaison between industry and government on R&D that would enhance the Nation's emergency preparedness and response capabilities.

The EMWG reports to the Oil and Natural Gas SCC and Chemical SCC chairs, and meets at least twice a year. In 2008 and 2009, the EMWG had numerous activities and achievements, including the development of a business continuity document and workshops focused on natural disasters and terrorist attacks.[22]

matters where pipeline safety and security overlap. DOE also works closely with the Federal Emergency Management Agency (FEMA) to address natural disasters and security issues related to the provision of energy and public safety. The U.S. Coast Guard (USCG) is responsible for protecting offshore oil and gas facilities, and for implementing regulations under the Maritime Transportation Security Act that impact Energy Sector facilities.[32] The USCG also has primary responsibility for problems at terminals and waterways. DOE is working with DHS to coordinate current and future threat identification and assessment, to map threats against U.S. vulnerabilities, to issue timely warnings, and to take preventive and protective action. DHS' Office of Cyber Security and Communications is working to address and enhance the security of all of the critical sectors' cyber infrastructure through such efforts as the Control Systems Security Program. Additionally, DHS is responsible for implementing chemical security regulations that will impact some important Energy Sector assets.

- **Department of the Interior (DOI)**. DOI's U.S. Geological Survey monitors coal mines and geothermal production areas and power plant siting. DOE, through the Power Marketing Administrations (PMAs), also coordinates power generation and river operations with DOI's Bureau of Reclamation on hydrogeneration projects. DOE also coordinates with DOI's Minerals Management Service (MMS), which manages the Nation's natural gas, oil, and other mineral resources on the Outer Continental Shelf.

---

[32] The USCG, Federal Energy Regulatory Commission (FERC), and DOT's Pipeline and Hazardous Materials Safety Administration (PHMSA) coordinate to address marine safety and security at LNG import facilities.

- **Department of State (DOS).** Energy is imported and exported each day. Under international agreements led by DOS and DHS, energy moves across U.S. borders with Canada and Mexico.

- **Department of Transportation (DOT).** The Energy Sector relies on pipelines, barges, tankers, railways, and highways to transport all raw and refined energy products. DOT's Pipeline and Hazardous Materials Safety Administration (PHMSA) coordinates activities regarding oil and natural gas pipelines, and is a member of the interagency committee charged with developing a memorandum of understanding (MOU) to facilitate prompt repair of oil and natural gas transmission pipelines. DOT's Maritime Administration (MARAD) programs promote the use of waterborne transportation and its seamless integration with other segments of the transportation system. MARAD also supports the Energy Sector by ensuring reserve shipping capacity is available in time of national emergency.

- **Environmental Protection Agency (EPA).** EPA is responsible for enforcement of the Clean Air Act. DOE coordinates with EPA during energy emergencies and supply disruptions to assess the availability of transportation and boutique fuels and the need for environmental fuel waivers. DOE also coordinates with EPA on air quality and fuel-related emissions.

- **Federal Energy Regulatory Commission (FERC).** FERC is an independent agency that regulates the interstate transmission of natural gas, oil, and electricity, as well as natural gas and hydropower projects. FERC oversees approval of electric reliability standards and enforcement of those standards, which are developed by NERC in its capacity as the Electric Reliability Organization (ERO) under the Energy Policy Act of 2005. FERC can also impose safety requirements to ensure or enhance the operational reliability of the LNG facilities within its jurisdiction. DOE coordinates with FERC on energy security issues.

- **Nuclear Regulatory Commission (NRC).** Energy partners continue to coordinate with NRC on energy security issues related to electricity generated by nuclear fission, relying on the experience gained from DOE's own operation of numerous nuclear facilities.

1.3.2.3 Relationships With State, Local, Tribal, and Territorial Agencies

States and local governments are crucial stakeholders in providing a secure and reliable energy infrastructure for the Nation. Their agencies are responsible for emergency planning and response, developing energy security and reliability policies and practices, and facilitating Energy Sector protection activities. Citizens turn to these organizations in times of crisis, and they play a significant role in preventing energy supply crises and mitigating the impacts of emergencies that do arise. DOE has established liaisons with State and local government agencies responsible for preventing and responding to energy disruptions. DOE continues to strengthen these relationships with the specific initiatives described in chapter 5. State and local organizations that play roles in Energy Sector security and assurance include the following:

- State government energy offices, represented by the National Association of State Energy Officials (NASEO), typically serve many energy-related functions at the State level, including coordinating responses to energy emergencies, developing energy emergency plans, and developing practices to improve energy security and reliability. This work is coordinated by NASEO's Energy Data and Security Committee.

- The Regional Consortium Coordinating Council was formed by DHS in 2008 to coordinate CIKR protection efforts within geographic areas and across jurisdictional boundaries. The mission of the RCCC is to strengthen regional collaborations that enhance protection, response, recovery, and resilience of the Nation's CIKR through collaboration among the Nation's regional consortia so that best practices, lessons learned, and other means of support can be shared.

- DHS has encouraged establishment of fusion centers. Many States and larger cities have created State and major urban area fusion centers to share information and intelligence within their jurisdictions as well as with the Federal Government. DHS is providing personnel with operational and intelligence skills to the fusion centers that support the unique needs of the locality. These personnel strive to:

  - Help the classified and unclassified information flow;

  - Provide expertise;

- Coordinate with local law enforcement and other agencies;

- Establish relationships with CIKR owners and operators; and

- Provide local awareness and access.

- State public utility commissions, represented by the National Association of Regulatory Utility Commissioners (NARUC), regulate utilities (energy, water, telecommunications) at the State level. In this role, the commissions are involved in cost-recovery issues (including energy security costs), energy supply curtailment plans, emergency response, cybersecurity, and CIP activities. NARUC's Committee on Critical Infrastructure is the focal point for this effort.

- Governors' offices and State legislators, represented by the National Governors Association (NGA) Center for Best Practices and the National Conference of State Legislatures (NCSL), respectively, develop policies that affect energy security and assurance and play major roles in responding to energy emergencies. These State-level decision makers coordinate with Federal and industry groups on energy security and emergency issues, and possess emergency authorities they may exercise to mitigate the impacts of energy crises.

- State Homeland Security Directors and their offices coordinate and conduct homeland security activities at the State level, including programs involving infrastructure protection and vulnerability analysis.

- State and local emergency management agencies, represented by the National Emergency Management Association (NEMA), and first responders prepare for and respond to all emergencies, including those with implications for the energy infrastructure. These agencies are on the front lines of emergency response at the State and local levels.

- Local governments and associations that represent them, such as the Public Technology Institute (PTI), comprise an extremely large set of stakeholders. They represent the interests of cities, towns, and municipalities in Energy Sector security, protection, and emergency preparedness.

- Tribal agencies play significant roles in electricity transmission corridors, especially in the Southwest, and in various energy supply resources, including coal and potentially in the growth of wind and other renewable energy sources.[33]

State and local governments are required under Federal homeland security funding guidance to implement the NIPP, as well as the National Response Framework (NRF) and National Incident Management System. As State and local governments develop their critical infrastructure plans, each Governor has designated a State Administrative Agency (SAA) to support development of homeland security strategies, implement strategic goals and objectives, and administer Federal preparedness assistance. In some cases, States have identified State agencies as sector leads. This would parallel the approach taken in HSPD-7 at the State level. For example, State public utility commissions are responsible for the cost recovery of utility investment in critical infrastructure, and many are responsible for emergency response and gas pipeline safety. Many State energy offices have expertise in the petroleum infrastructure, monitor petroleum supply and demand, and provide for emergency response as well.

At the national level, the Energy Emergency Assurance Coordinators (EEAC) system is a cooperative effort among NASEO, NARUC, NCSL, NGA's Center for Best Practices, PTI, and DOE's Office of Electricity Delivery and Energy Reliability (OE)/ Infrastructure Security and Energy Restoration Division (ISER). The system establishes a secure cooperative communications environment for State and local government personnel with access to information on energy supply, demand, pricing, and infrastructure. Designated members have expertise in electricity, petroleum, and natural gas. The current membership is composed of representatives from State energy offices, public utility commissions, State legislatures, emergency management agencies, homeland security offices, and governors' offices. The EEAC system is housed on DOE's ISERnet Web site.[34]

---

[33] See Council of Energy Resource Tribes at **www.certredearth.com**.

[34] ISERnet is an Internet community of Federal, State, and local government and industry professionals who share in the effort to protect CIKR in the Energy Sector and ensure a secure and reliable flow of energy. DOE's Office of Electricity Delivery and Energy Reliability/Infrastructure Security and Energy Restoration established this secure communication environment to address energy emergencies and supply disruptions and share timely information. The site contains two separate systems: the EEAC system for State and local governments, and the EIAC system for industry personnel.

Critical Infrastructure Protection Advisory Council (CIPAC). DOE also works in partnership with CIPAC, established by DHS as part of the NIPP. CIPAC facilitates interaction among government representatives and representatives of CIKR owners and operators in each sector.

Information Sharing and Analysis Center. DOE collaborates with the sector's use of the Electricity Sector Information Sharing and Analysis Center (ESISAC)[35] and the Homeland Security Information Network (HSIN).[36] (See chapter 5 for a more complete description.) ESISAC and HSIN provide mechanisms by which the energy industry can share and analyze important information about vulnerabilities, threats, intrusions, and anomalies, and through which it can communicate with and provide support to the Federal Government. Both ESISAC and ONG-HSIN can be used to share information with other critical infrastructures. In addition, DOE's secure ISERnet Web site contains the Energy Industry Assurance Coordinators (EIAC) system, a database of key industry personnel who can exchange information with DOE during energy emergencies. The site provides threat awareness and relevant security analyses and presentations.

1.4 Value Proposition

Efficiently and effectively securing the Energy Sector necessitates significant investment from all sector partners. These investments require expenditures of time, energy, money, and other resources. While these expenditures typically are executively or legislatively mandated for government, private sector participation is mostly voluntary. Beyond existing regulatory requirements, participation by the private sector has been significant in the Energy Sector. Reasons for private sector partners to participate include opportunities to:

- Complement existing trade association and sector activities and programs, both voluntary and regulated.

- Share credible, timely, actionable threat information and predictive/trend analyses where possible.

- Apply a risk-based and prudent business approach for protecting assets that builds on existing industry practices and methodologies.

- Support flexible allocation of protective resources based on threats, consequences, and vulnerabilities.

- Improve risk management through exposure to effective practices and risk management tools.

- Provide a forum for reaching out to peers and addressing interdependencies.

- Provide a platform for coordination and communication between government and industry regarding protective actions and risk management activities.

- Build and further strengthen existing trusted relationships with private and public sector partners.

- Inform government regarding impediments to protecting or recovery of energy assets.

- Promote improved coordination, consolidation, and prioritization of multiple (and sometimes competing) Federal initiatives involving the Energy Sector, with input and assistance from the Energy Sector GCC.

[35] ESISAC, **www.esisac.com**.

[36] HSIN is managed by the National Operations Center, **www.dhs.gov/dhspublic/display?theme=30&content=3813. ONG-HSIN** replaced ESISAC in August 2006.

2. Identify Assets, Systems, and Networks

Figure 2-1: Identify Assets, Systems, and Networks

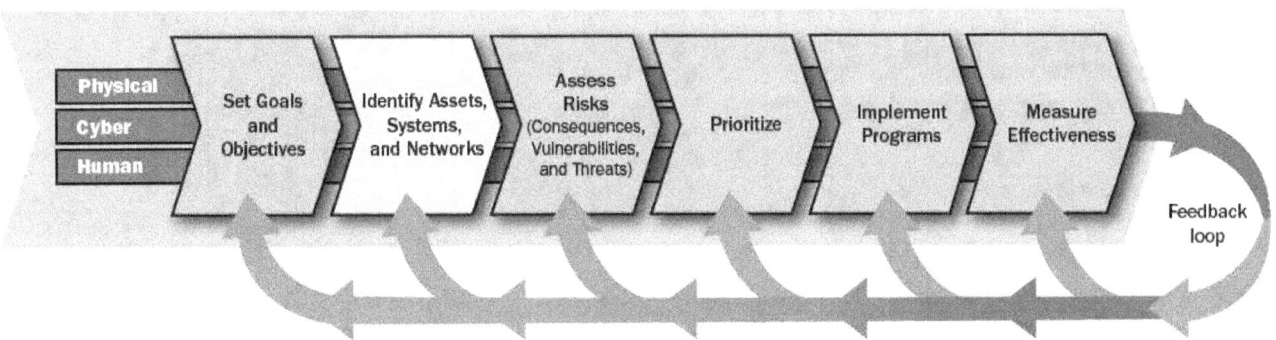

Continuous improvement to enhance protection of CIKR

This chapter discusses the ongoing efforts by industry, and as appropriate by government partners, to identify Energy Sector assets, systems, and networks that could, if compromised, result in significant economic damage or human casualty. It also discusses the relevant information parameters and existing data sources available to the Energy Sector in its efforts to conduct risk management activities and protect infrastructure assets and systems.

2.1 Defining Information Parameters

2.1.1 Energy Assets and Systems

Broadly speaking, HSPD-7 defines the Energy Sector as the Nation's electric system (excluding nuclear power plants and hydroelectric dams), natural gas system, and petroleum/petroleum product systems. Figure 2-2 describes the operation of the electric grids in North America. As discussed in chapter 1, these three energy systems are highly interdependent (e.g., natural gas is a significant fuel for electric generation) and are critical for other infrastructure sectors, including Communications, Water, Chemical, Information Technology, and Transportation Systems. Each of these interdependent energy systems consists of many individual assets. In some cases these assets may be highly important, but their importance varies dramatically depending on factors such as time of day, time of year, and system conditions. From a reliability and security perspective, systems are the critical characteristic of the Energy Sector.

While the power system in North America is commonly referred to as "the grid," there are actually four distinct power grids or "interconnections." The Eastern Interconnection includes the eastern two-thirds of the continental United States and Canada from Saskatchewan east to the Maritime Provinces. This excludes Quebec Province, which is its own interconnection, the fourth in North America. The Western Interconnection includes the western one-third of the continental United States (excluding Alaska), the Canadian provinces of Alberta and British Columbia, and a portion of Baja California Norte, Mexico. The third interconnection comprises most of the State of Texas. The interconnections are electrically independent from each other except for a few direct current (DC) ties that link them. Within each interconnection, electricity is used the instant it is produced and flows over virtually all transmission lines from generators to loads.

The four power grids form an integrated system that has been described as the world's largest machine. It is made up of hundreds of thousands of interconnected generators, transmission lines, and substations. Each of these individual components is designed and operated within the parameters necessary to assure integrated grid reliability. Reliable operation of the power grid is achieved by addressing two fundamental characteristics of electricity.

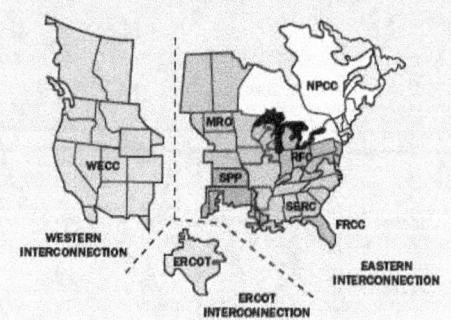

The electricity grid that serves the continental United States and Canada is actually four separate systems.

First, electricity flows at close to the speed of light and is not economically storable in large quantities. Therefore, electricity must be used the instant it is produced and the system must be managed every second of the day to monitor and respond to changes very quickly.

Second, electricity flows freely along all available alternating current (AC) paths from the generators to the loads according to the laws of physics, dividing among all connected flow paths in the network. These multiple paths provide the resilience necessary to respond instantly to both planned and unexpected equipment outages in the system.

Maintaining reliability requires trained and skilled operators, sophisticated computers and communications, and careful planning and design. To ensure the reliability of the four grids, NERC and its eight Regional Reliability Councils have developed system operating and planning standards, based on seven key concepts, for ensuring the reliability of the four grids:

1. Balance power generation and demand continuously.

2. Balance reactive power supply and demand to maintain scheduled voltages.

3. Monitor flows over transmission lines and other facilities to ensure that thermal (heating) limits are not exceeded.

4. Keep the system in a stable condition.

5. Operate the system so that it remains in a reliable condition even if a contingency occurs, such as the loss of a key generator or transmission facility (the "N-1 criterion").

6. Plan, design, and maintain the system to operate reliably.

7. Prepare for and respond to emergencies.

Planning and operating standards are reinforced through compliance audits, sanctions, and penalties that will be enforceable across North America as NERC evolves to fulfill its role as the ERO. Some State public utility commissions may also have a role in assuring reliable operation of the power grid.

2.1.2 Defining Energy Asset and System Parameters

The Energy Sector has identified six general asset or system characteristics that are important parameters for evaluating the vulnerabilities of the Energy Sector infrastructure and developing risk management programs.

- **Physical and location attributes**. Consideration of these assists the Energy Sector in developing consequence, vulnerability, and protective strategies.

- **Cyber attributes**. Like physical attributes, these assist the Energy Sector to evaluate consequences and vulnerabilities, and develop protective strategies. Cyber systems that link and help monitor and control the energy systems are increasingly recognized as a potential vulnerability.

- **Volumetric or throughput attributes**. These define the extent of any damage, depending on the utilized capacity of the system, or points where the system may be capacity constrained.

- **Temporal/load profile attributes**. The Energy Sector has a strong temporal or time-dependent dimension affected by the season of the year and/or time of day.

- **Human attributes**. Highly trained and skilled personnel are key factors in a comprehensive Energy Sector security plan. The availability of skilled and experienced technical talent is a concern in the Energy Sector. Sustaining essential technical knowledge is critical to maintaining the sector's safety, reliability, and security.

- **Importance of an asset or system to the energy network**. Disruption of a particular gas pipeline or storage facility could impact the ability of numerous power generation assets to function because of lack of fuel, which could in turn affect key telecommunications facilities, water treatment facilities, transportation facilities, or other critical infrastructure.

2.1.3 Information Collection and Sharing

The Energy Sector has considerable data available to support a wide range of consequence, risk, and vulnerability assessments. The data is collected and used by owners, operators, trade associations, and a variety of industry organizations such as NERC, the American Gas Association (AGA), and American Petroleum Institute (API). In addition, the Government collects a wide variety of Energy Sector information, principally through the authorities of various Federal agencies[37] and—at the State and local levels—through authorities of public utility commissions, State energy offices, and State and local homeland security initiatives (appendix 7, table A7-1). Established communication links also exist between Federal, State, and local government representatives and industry. However, the amount of Energy Sector cyber data is limited.

During times of increased security posture or emergency situations, the best information sources are the trusted relationships between government and industry. Such relationships ensure that necessary information is provided when and where it is needed and can be directly applied to protect and recover key energy infrastructure and resources. Established relationships between industry and all levels of government and other key stakeholders will continue to facilitate information flow, when necessary, through HSIN and other information-sharing mechanisms. Further, working with the Department of Energy, sector partners will continue to communicate with DHS regarding additional needs, information resources, and database approaches required to support DHS programs. State energy emergency preparedness and response plans highlight the identification of assets and the role of State government officials, in conjunction with their private sector counterparts, in addressing various levels of an energy emergency.

The Energy Sector owners and operators have a long history of mutual aid and support that can be relied on in emergency situations. This aid is largely focused on emergency response and recovery to support restoration of service to customers. Regional planning groups in the natural gas and electricity industries plan for regional reliability and often conduct exercises to prepare

---

[37] For example, FERC, EIA, DOE, DOT, DHS, TSA, and USCG.

for energy emergencies. States also conduct regional energy emergency exercises involving the private sector to assure coordinated responses across State borders and with the private sector.

The goal of the National Cyber Security Division's Control Systems Security Program (CSSP) is to reduce industrial control system risks within and across all CIKR sectors by coordinating efforts among Federal, State, local, and tribal governments, as well as industrial control systems owners, operators and vendors. The CSSP coordinates activities to reduce the likelihood of success and severity of impact of a cyber attack against critical infrastructure control systems through risk mitigation activities. An Industrial Control Systems-Computer Emergency Response Team (ICS-CERT) has been created in DHS. The ICS-CERT has an enormous and challenging mission to look across all of the sectors' control systems to study vulnerabilities, provide assessments and mitigations, and share information.

2.1.4 Existing Energy Sector Information Resources

As stated previously, the Energy Sector has substantial information sources available to support CIKR protection, planning, and analysis (appendix 8). The following sections describe the types of information used by the Energy Sector.

2.1.4.1 Electric Generation and Transmission Information

Electric generation and transmission assets are grouped into existing and new plants and facilities. Because of the long lead times to build a new power plant or transmission line and bring it on line, tracking of new facilities in various stages of development is performed by the industry. Major attributes include location, capacity, and ramp-up or black start times, as well as electrical location on the grid (in terms of voltage support and similar grid stability metrics). These attributes relate directly to operators' abilities to maintain power production to meet demand throughout both scheduled and unscheduled plant outages.

2.1.4.2 Petroleum Asset Information

Physical petroleum asset data, including location and throughput data, are maintained by both industry and government. These data are important in assessing the consequences and vulnerability of the various types of petroleum assets. As with electricity, data on petroleum control systems and markets/trading platforms are also maintained.

2.1.4.3 Natural Gas Asset Information

Government and industry both maintain natural gas asset data. Natural gas systems also employ SCADA-type control systems and markets/trading platforms for which asset data are maintained. Natural gas markets have existed for some time, and both physical and financial products are traded. A key platform is the New York Mercantile Exchange (NYMEX).

FERC requires the annual filing of system flow diagrams by jurisdictional companies.[38] These filings contain data for facilities that were installed or operated during the reporting year and include miles of pipeline, diameter of each section, maximum allowable operating pressures of each segment, direction of flow, total horsepower at each compressor station, daily and seasonal withdrawal volumes at each storage field, and volume delivered to each customer.

Another filing requirement instructs jurisdictional companies to notify FERC of all serious service interruptions lasting longer than three hours.[39] Reports must be filed at the earliest possible time following the interruption and must include the location, time, and number of customers affected, as well as any emergency measures taken to remedy the situation.

2.1.4.4 Protection of Collected Data

Energy Sector owners and operators expect that all data and information voluntarily provided to DHS or DOE by industry will be protected from release by Protected Critical Infrastructure Information (PCII) or other appropriate classification procedures.

---

[38] As specified in 18 CFR 260.8.

[39] As specified in 18 CFR 260.9.

DOE has been accredited to receive PCII information. DOE works with the PCII Program Office within the DHS Office of Infrastructure Protection (IP) to apply provisions of the CII Act—as well as implementing regulations contained in 6 CFR Part 29—to critical infrastructure information that is not customarily in the public domain and is voluntarily submitted to DHS or to DOE. Other government sector partners also work to protect sensitive information from unintended release. DOE is committed to protecting any sensitive information that it receives from sector partners. Public and private partners throughout the Energy Sector work with State, local, and tribal authorities to ensure that information provided to those non-Federal authorities is also appropriately protected from release and not used for purposes other than infrastructure protection and recovery. Through NARUC, States are developing models for information sharing and protection in the State regulatory context, and public utility commissions are engaging in training and network-building that will enable each State to provide the right information to the right parties when needed.

2.2 Collecting Infrastructure Information

Large CIP-focused data collection efforts on the part of government agencies are not required because the sector already has considerable data to help analyze consequences and vulnerabilities and to develop protective and resilience strategies. However, when appropriate, DOE will work with sector partners to obtain and appropriately protect additional information, cybersecurity, and energy system and resilience issues. The Cyberspace Policy Review: Assuring a Trusted and Resilient Information and Communications Infrastructure[40] called for the development of unified Federal policy guidance for cybersecurity-related activities. DOE and energy sector partners will also work and coordinate with other sectors where dependencies and interdependencies exist. DOE will work with DHS, DoD, FERC, and other government partners to ensure legal and policy frameworks are in place to reduce duplication of data requests. Through trade associations and State and local efforts, sector partners engage regularly with other key sectors that rely on energy or on which they rely.

For State and local efforts, some additional information may also be needed on critical energy infrastructure in their jurisdictions so that they understand risk, vulnerabilities, and consequences, and can properly set their priorities for protective measures that will support and complement the private sector efforts.

2.3 Verifying and Updating Infrastructure Information

Many of the existing data used by DOE and sector partners are already subject to verification and validation protocols. For example, EIA maintains a rigorous data verification and validation program for the data it collects from industry. Many State commissions, FERC, and NRC also conduct data and management audits of reporting companies because the data are used for regulatory and ratemaking purposes. TSA has an ongoing program in which data on pipeline security programs are collected and evaluated. Where existing data verification processes are deemed inadequate, the DOE will work with NIPP participants to create expert groups to identify and implement appropriate processes, including processes to verify cyber-related data.

DOE will work with government agencies and asset owners and operators to ensure the data used for CIP purposes are verified, fill a clearly identified void, meet mutually agreed-upon levels of accuracy, and are essential to energy infrastructure protection, restoration, and recovery. Products from these efforts will be shared with sector partners as appropriate and protected from unintentional release. Confidential and proprietary information will be protected from disclosure. In emergencies or crises, trusted communication channels among sector partners will be engaged to ensure that the data collected is relevant.

DOE will work with sector partners as needed to update key energy asset and infrastructure data, including data on cyber-related assets in cooperation with DHS and other Federal agencies.

---

[40] Cyberspace Policy Review: Assuring a Trusted and Resilient Information and Communications Infrastructure, 2009, **http://www.whitehouse.gov/assets/documents/ Cyberspace_Policy_Review_final.pdf**.

3. Assess Risks

Figure 3-1: Assess Risks

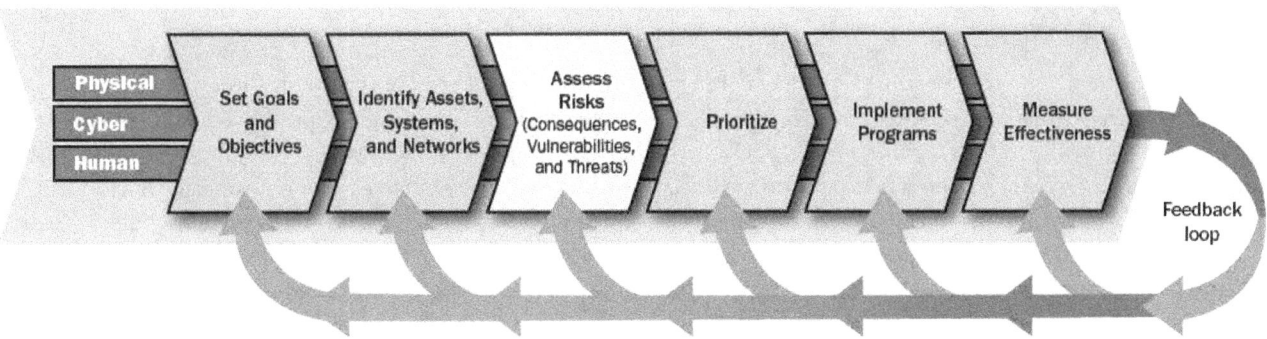

Continuous improvement to enhance protection of CIKR

This chapter describes the current approaches being used in the Energy Sector for assessing risk. As defined in the NIPP, risk is a measure of potential harm that encompasses threat, vulnerability, and consequence. That is:

$$\text{Risk (R)} = f(C, T, V)$$

where an asset's risk is a function of the likely consequences (C) of a disruption or successful attack; the likelihood of a disruption or attack on the asset, often referred to as the threat (T) to the asset or the asset's attractiveness; and the asset's vulnerability (V) to a disruption or attack. As discussed in the sections below, a variety of approaches are used in the Energy Sector that apply this widely accepted risk management principle to assess risk.

3.1 Use of Risk Assessment in the Sector

Sector owners and operators have extensive experience in developing and applying facility and system risk assessment methodologies as well as prioritizing assets for protection. Risk assessment methodologies have been developed by a variety of sector partners, including: individual energy companies that own and operate sector assets, professional and trade associations, academic institutions, research centers, and DOE. Such an approach is integral to DOE's ability to meet its longstanding responsibilities for safety and security, and to implement its CIP program for the Energy Sector.

Various risk assessment methodologies are used to address the diversity of assets in the Energy Sector. Some methodologies are tailored to a specific segment of the sector (e.g., electricity, oil, natural gas, or their system components), while others are used to assess risks at the system or sector level. In addition, some have broad applicability that extends across multiple CIKR sectors.

Many of the methodologies used in the Energy Sector include dependencies and interdependencies among infrastructures. The energy industry sponsors and participates in regional and national planning activities. Such activities are designed to identify and analyze system and interdependency considerations that transcend individual companies, considerations that may also be used by DHS to prioritize efforts during national emergencies. Through the NIPP partnership, Energy Sector participants have been actively engaged in exercises to develop response strategies involving multiple sectors, agencies, companies, and governmental entities. The sector will continue to develop ties to other sectors and to explore the extent and importance of interdependencies.

The broad range of methods used by the Energy Sector to assess risk is also a function of the international scope of the sector's assets, supply chains, and products. Many energy companies are global and have extensive experience in dealing with a wide variety of natural and manmade threats. This experience has resulted in effective ways to prioritize infrastructure protection and resilience investments based on risk. It has also highlighted the importance of interdependencies within the sector as well as among the other CIKR sectors.

DOE, in cooperation with sector partners, has undertaken programs to assess the risks of key energy infrastructure assets and to provide technology, tools, and expertise to other Federal, State, and local organizations and the private sector. These programs are designed to assist all entities within the energy infrastructure in securing systems against physical and cyber attacks. One example is the Energy Sector Control Systems Working Group, utilizing the Energy Control Systems Roadmap, which is a DOE-led collaborative effort that helps the Energy Sector address cybersecurity issues. Other products include vulnerability and risk assessment-related methodologies, checklists, lessons learned, support for policy analysis, and guidelines for various types of assets. The programs have also established partnerships with infrastructure owners/operators, State and local governments, and a wide range of industry associations.

DOE in cooperation with DHS and sector partners is working to:

- Strengthen the energy industry's cyber capabilities by establishing a broad-based public-private partnership for collaboration and cooperation;

- Enhance electric energy infrastructure reliability and cybersecurity solutions development;

- Assist in creating a framework to identify and prepare for near term and future challenges to grid reliability, and;

- Stimulate support and interaction with key grid suppliers and vendors.

DOE, in partnership with energy industry owners and operators, has also worked closely with DHS in developing and transferring risk assessment methodologies. The sector has participated in DHS's Buffer Zone Protection Program (BZPP) and Site Assistance Visit (SAV) Program and has collaborated with the Protective Security Advisors (PSAs) in the Enhanced Critical Infrastructure Protection (ECIP) Initiative. The PSAs' mission is to identify, assess, monitor, and minimize risks to CIKR assets at the local or district level. Spread across regions and metropolitan areas throughout the Nation, PSAs foster improved coordination and partnership between DHS and State, local, tribal, and territorial authorities, as well as the private sector. Such efforts enable PSAs to provide a local perspective to the national risk picture, as well as a Federal resource to CIKR owners and operators and local law enforcement. DOE and DHS will work together to coordinate the PSAs' physical security focus with a broader effort to examine system level supply chain and cyber risks. Prior to their release, products will be reviewed by sector partners to ensure they are useful. These efforts seek to develop energy security baselines and identify trends and possible concerns for industry use. Given the diversity of facilities in the Energy Sector and the wide range of methodologies being used to assess risk successfully, a "one size fits all" risk assessment solution is not appropriate.

Voluntary cooperative efforts with sector partners support Energy SSP goals by partnering with the industry to develop the information requirements and metrics necessary to conduct energy system-level reliability impact analysis. The longer term goals are to streamline information gathering and to reduce duplication of reporting requests and undue burden on industry. The resulting analysis will provide industry participants and DOE with information on energy system-level supply chain issues, optimal risk mitigation activities, and enhanced response and recovery after an energy event—regardless of the cause. These will assist government and industry efforts to identify systemic problems and to examine supply chain considerations and dependency issues that may have an energy system-wide impact.

To supplement the current screening processes used by industry, the public and private sector partners have collaborated with the DHS in the implementation of the Chemical Facility Anti-Terrorism Standards (CFATS) rule which covers a number of Energy Sector assets. The CFATS program is a regulatory framework that DHS uses to advance the security of high-risk chemical facilities. Authorized by section 550 of the Homeland Security Appropriations Act of 2007, DHS created CFATS to identify, assess, and ensure effective security at high-risk chemical facilities. DHS published a proposed rule for public comment in December 2006. The CFATS Interim Final Rule was published on April 9, 2007 and went into effect on June 8, 2007. The CFATS list of "chemicals of interest" contains a number of chemicals that are handled or used in various types of energy infrastructure, including gasoline, propane, and ethanol. For this reason, CFATS may be applicable to certain energy facilities. DHS has identified more than 6,000 chemical facilities in the preliminary tiering, including some energy facilities. However, the final tiering, total number, and location of energy facilities that fall under the CFATS regulations have not been finalized – and will change over time as the facilities change.

The NIPP[41] defines a set of baseline criteria for the methodologies used to support all levels of comparative risk analysis. Sector partners will consider such criteria through CIPAC as the sector works with public sector partners to evaluate how best to improve these methodologies and move forward with the vulnerability and risk assessments that will support DHS' national risk analysis goals. DOE and sector partners agree with DHS' stated objective of using previously performed assessment results whenever possible to support such analysis.

3.2 Screening Infrastructure

As discussed in chapter 1, the Energy Sector consists of many millions of electricity, oil, and natural gas assets that are connected by systems and networks. Screening methodologies help identify which assets are significant for further assessment. That is, they enable a determination of the need for a more detailed vulnerability or risk assessment. Numerous energy facilities and assets are spread throughout the Nation, many of which may pose little or no security risk. It is neither practical nor financially responsible to perform comprehensive risk assessments on all assets and facilities, especially as limited resources are available to address their security. Thus, as a precursor to in-depth risk assessment efforts, screening is used to identify which facilities warrant expenditure of additional resources.

Energy companies use many screening approaches to prioritize facilities for more rigorous assessments. These approaches commonly focus on health and safety consequences as well as broad-based economic consequences. Energy industry associations have developed and disseminated security guidelines to help screen assets, including:

- Security Vulnerability Assessment Methodology for the Petroleum and Petrochemical Industries, Second Edition, API, and National Petrochemical & Refiners Association (NPRA).[42]

- Security Guidelines for the Petroleum Industry, API.

---

[41] See NIPP, appendix 3A.

[42] Available at **http://new.api.org/policy/otherissues/upload/SVA_E2.pdf**.

- Security Guidelines: Natural Gas Industry Transmission and Distribution, AGA, Interstate Natural Gas Association of America (INGAA), and American Public Gas Association (APGA).

- TSA Pipeline Security Guidelines, Transportation Security Administration.

- Security Guidelines for the Electricity Sector, NERC.[43] (Note: Like other guidelines in the Energy Sector, these continue to evolve as the threats and challenges to the electric infrastructure and the tools used to address them continue to develop.)

- Critical Infrastructure Protection (CIP) Reliability Standards, CIP-002-1 through CIP-009-1, NERC, approved by FERC. Version 2 CIP Reliability Standards CIP-002-2 through CIP-009-2, NERC, approved by FERC.[44] (Note: The CIP Reliability Standards provide a framework for identification and protection of critical cyber assets to support reliable operation of the bulk electric system.)

Electric grid operators utilize their energy management systems to run sophisticated contingency analysis programs every 5 to 10 seconds to identify the most critical components of the electric grid. The operators are always aware of the critical components, as well as the consequences if a key component is removed from service, and operate the system to mitigate the loss of any key components.

In addition to the current screening processes used by industry, DHS, in conjunction with industry, has developed "Top Screens" for petroleum refining and LNG facilities.

Industry, in cooperation with governmental Energy Sector partners, continues to discuss common approaches and next steps to refine approaches and to share experiences It also continues to share experiences, commonalities, and effective practices in the use of physical and cyber security tools for the assessment of potential risks and vulnerabilities. These approaches involve industry security committees and experts as well as SCCs and key government participants.

3.3 Assessing Consequences

The potential physical and cyber consequences of any incident, including terrorist attacks and natural or manmade disasters, are the primary consideration in risk assessment. In the context of the NIPP, consequence is measured as the range of loss or damage that can be expected.

The consequences that are considered for the national-level comparative risk assessment are based on the criteria set forth in HSPD-7. These criteria can be divided into four main categories:

- **Human Impact**: Effect on human life and physical well-being (e.g., fatalities, injuries).

- **Economic Impact**: Direct and indirect effects on the economy (e.g., costs resulting from disruption of products or services, costs to respond to and recover from the disruption, costs to rebuild the asset, and long-term costs due to environmental damage).

- **Impact on Public Confidence**: Effect on public morale and confidence in national economic and political institutions.

- **Impact on Government Capability**: Effect on the government's ability to maintain order, deliver minimum essential public services, ensure public health and safety, and carry out national security-related missions.

An assessment of all categories of consequence may be beyond the capabilities available for a given risk analysis. Most Energy Sector assets are not associated with the possibility of mass casualties, but may have economic and long-term health and safety

---

[43] Available at **http://www.esisac.net/library-guidelines.htm**.

[44] Available at **http://www.nerc.com/page.php?cid=2|20**.

implications if disrupted. However, the redundancy of system-critical facilities and overall system resilience minimize the potential for such consequences.

The complexity, diversity, and interconnectedness of the Energy Sector dictate the need for assessing consequences at many different levels of detail:

- Asset or facility level.

- System, sector, and urban area level.

- Regional and/or national level.

These assessments must consider both physical and cyber interdependencies within the Energy Sector and among the other CIKR sectors at all levels. These interdependencies may have national, regional, State, and/or local implications and are considered to be an essential element of a comprehensive examination of physical and cyber vulnerabilities.

DOE, as the Energy SSA, and the Energy Sector SCCs coordinates with DHS, DOT, FERC and other Federal organizations with responsibilities under HSPD-7 as appropriate to ensure that assessments are conducted in a timely manner. Increasing cooperation and coordination between DOE and States is currently facilitated by ARRA funding granted to States and localities to further develop their energy security planning.

3.4 Assessing Threats

The Energy Sector takes a broad view of threat analysis, one that encompasses natural events, criminal acts, insider threats, and foreign and domestic terrorism. Natural events are typically addressed as part of emergency response and business continuity planning. In the context of risk assessment, the threat component is calculated based on the likelihood that an asset will be disrupted or attacked. Such information is essential for conducting meaningful vulnerability and risk assessments. Therefore, relevant and timely threat information must be disseminated whenever possible. A number of sector representatives hold national security clearances that facilitate the sharing of classified threat information. In addition, the ES-ISAC facilitates communications between Electricity subsector participants, the Federal Government, and other critical infrastructures, and is a conduit for disseminating sensitive threat and incident information. A number of State and local authorities, with DHS support, have created fusion centers that combine relevant law enforcement and intelligence information analysis and coordinate security measures to reduce threats in their respective communities.

Asset owners and operators must rely on threat information from DHS and Federal, State, and local law enforcement organizations in order to assess the relative risk associated with a given asset. The DHS Homeland Infrastructure Threat and Risk Analysis Center (HITRAC), which conducts integrated threat analysis for all CIKR sectors, works in partnership with owners and operators and other Federal, State, and local government agencies to ensure that suitable threat information is made available. Furthermore, the same level of partnership must exist within all levels of Federal, State, and local law enforcement.

The following types of threat products provided by HITRAC are used to support planning activities in the Energy Sector:

- **Common Threat Scenarios**, which present methods and tactics that could be employed in attacks against the U.S. infrastructure.

- **General Threat Environment Assessments**, which are sector-specific threat products that include known terrorist threat information and long-term strategic assessments and trend analyses of the evolving threats to the sector's critical infrastructure.

- **Specific Threat Information**, which is critical infrastructure-specific information based on real-time intelligence, and drives short-term measures to mitigate risk.

In addition to these products, the Energy Sector further benefits from the continuation of:

- Periodic conference calls with asset owners and operators to relay recently reported suspicious activities near energy facilities and other pertinent unclassified threat-related information.

- Reports analyzing suspicious activities said to have occurred near energy facilities.

- Classified threat briefings for representatives of the energy industry. Various Federal agencies would use these briefings to inform industry representatives about general and specific threats associated with the Energy Sector, as well as the overall threat of terrorism to the Nation. These briefings should include representatives from the appropriate elements of the Intelligence Community including the Office of the Director of National Intelligence (ODNI), DHS, CIA, DoD, DOE, and FBI.

- Improved communications and increased participation with regional, State, and local joint terrorism task forces and organizations.

- Interagency forums and workgroups, such as the Pacific Northwest Economic Region (PNWER), and other State and local information-sharing, emergency-planning, and exercise efforts that benefit the Energy Sector as well as other participating sectors.

- Information on domestic and foreign cyber threats, which are increasingly seen as having the potential to target the Energy Sector. The sector coordinates with the Cross-Sector Cyber Security Working Group, USCERT, HITRAC, and NCSD to identify and mitigate potential and actual cyber threats and vulnerabilities.

- Discussion of potentially high-impact but low-frequency (HILF) threats, such as electromagnetic pulse (EMP) caused by nuclear weapons, or solar/geomagnetic sources. The industry is also working to prepare for possible coordinated physical or cyber attacks, or for a major pandemic as shown in figure 3-2.

- These forums and materials provide insights to sector partners regarding the overall threat to the energy industry. More specifically, they help energy facilities, local law enforcement, and others to be more aware of potential indicators of terrorist and/or criminal activity.

3.5 Assessing Vulnerabilities

Vulnerabilities are the characteristics of an asset, system, or network's design, location, security posture, process, or operation that render it susceptible to destruction, incapacitation, or exploitation by mechanical failures, natural hazards, terrorist attacks, or other malicious acts. Vulnerability assessments identify areas of weakness that could result in consequences of concern, taking into account intrinsic structural weaknesses, protective measures, resilience, and redundancies.

Historically, the Energy Sector has been proactive in developing and applying vulnerability assessment methodologies tailored to its assets and systems. However, no single vulnerability tool or assessment methodology is universally applicable. Individual energy companies use assessment tools that are developed by professional and trade associations, Federal organizations, government laboratories, and private sector firms. The number of tools in use is large, and the vast majority of significant facilities in the Energy Sector have already undergone assessments using one or more of these tools.

Sector owners and operators have also participated in DHS/DOE-led SAVs. The SAVs are facility vulnerability assessments focused on identifying security gaps and recommending protective measures. SAVs are conducted by the DHS Protective Security Coordination Division's (PSCD) Vulnerability Assessment Branch. PSCD coordinates with PSAs from the DHS Field Operations Branch, other Federal, State, local, territorial, and tribal entities and CIKR owners and operators. During these visits, DHS professionals and other subject-matter experts assist asset owners/operators in assessing and characterizing vulnerabilities at their critical infrastructure sites. The visits are designed to facilitate vulnerability identification and mitigation discussions between government and industry. They also help DHS identify vulnerabilities that are common to specific asset types, subsectors, and sectors. At the conclusion of a SAV, DHS representatives brief the asset owner/operator on identified vulnerabilities

Figure 3-2: Pandemic Influenza Planning

Although the H1N1 "swine flu" outbreak of spring 2009 heightened its urgency, pandemic influenza planning is nothing new. Members of the Energy Sector–both individually and collectively–have been preparing for a possible influenza pandemic for some time. DOE has been collaborating with its sector partners at various levels. These partners include: CIKR owners and operators; key energy trade associations (NERC, EEI, API, and AGA); Federal agencies (DHS, Department of Health and Human Services (HHS), and Centers for Disease Control and Prevention (CDC)); and State and local governments. Such sector partnerships enable timely dissemination of information and enhance awareness of the full range of threats to CIKR.

For CIKR owners and operators, preparation for pandemic influenza is closely linked to business continuity planning. Many Energy CIKR owners and operators have already integrated the potential impacts of pandemic influenza into their business continuity plans; those who have not are encouraged to do so. In the face of avian flu and H1N1, the Energy Sector has worked through its trade organizations to improve pandemic planning. It has developed guides, exercises, working groups, and points-of-contact. Examples of pandemic reference guides include:

· The Electricity Subsector Pandemic Influenza Guideline (DHS)

· The Oil and Natural Gas Subsector Pandemic Influenza Guideline (DHS)

· Electricity Subsector Influenza Pandemic Planning, Preparation, and Response Reference Guide (NERC)

· Electric Utilities and Pandemic Planning (EEI)

and protective measure options that are being used throughout the sector. The SAV team also authors a classified or unclassified report for the facility. The information learned at these site visits is used to develop Characteristics and Common Vulnerabilities Reports for different sectors and subsectors.

Energy Sector owners and operators as well as government sector partners also face vulnerabilities as a result of an aging workforce. The sector has taken proactive measures to address the prospective shortage of trained personnel in the industry. Both the Electricity and Oil and Natural Gas subsectors face the question of how to provide the manpower and expertise needed to meet future energy demands. As energy demand continues to increase, and energy infrastructure continues to age, "the loss of industry workers and their years of accumulated expertise due to retirements is a serious threat to the bulk power system reliability, exacerbated by the lack of new recruits entering the field."[45] Such concern was particularly heightened during the contingency planning for a possible influenza pandemic.

A group of energy utilities and their associations-EEI, AGA, the Nuclear Energy Institute (NEI), and NRECA-formed a non-profit consortium called the Center for Energy Workforce Development (CEWD).[46] Teaming with educational institutions and the workforce system, CEWD helps utilities work together to create solutions for the industry's need for a qualified, diverse workforce.

---

[45] 2007 Long-Term Reliability Assessment, NERC, at **http://www.nerc.com/files/LTRA2007.pdf**.

[46] The Center for Energy Workforce Development (CEWD), at **http://www.cewd.org/index.asp**.

4. Prioritize Infrastructure

Figure 4-1: Prioritize

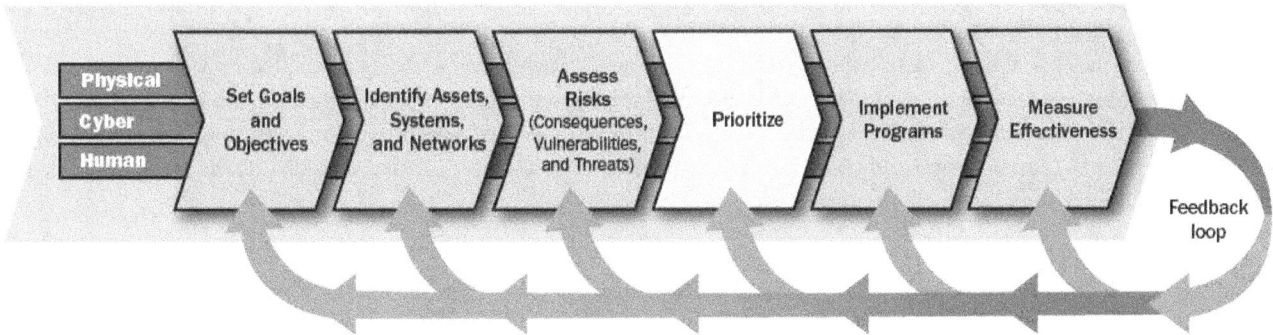

Continuous improvement to enhance protection of CIKR

As explained in previous chapters, the Energy Sector is characterized by large networks as opposed to discrete assets. These networks are designed to operate with certain levels of reliability, even if portions of them (discrete components, or assets) are out of service.

The importance of many of the individual components in the network is highly variable, depending upon location, time of day, day of the week, month of the year, and many other variables. What might be a critical asset on a Monday morning in January may not be critical on a Saturday afternoon in June.

Owners and operators of Energy Sector assets and networks have screening processes to identify internal priorities related to business conditions and supply/grid reliability to help them ensure continuity of operations. From a grid perspective, the Nation's oil and natural gas pipeline systems and electricity grid are designed and operated with built-in redundancy to ensure a certain degree of reliability and resilience. Industry planning criteria assume a local grid area can be operated even if one asset is out of service. In addition, during unforeseen events, the industry provides mutual aid to assist in emergency response and prompt restoration[47] (See chapter 5).

NERC and regional reliability councils for the electricity industry continuously evaluate network reliability. Their functions are well developed and understood, and the United States has among the most reliable electric and natural gas grids in the world.

---

[47] The effectiveness of mutual aid agreements can be significantly affected by the nature of an event. Mutual aid partners could also be affected by an event, and a utility might have to go outside the region to obtain aid. It should also be noted that response and restoration may be affected by shortages in critical components, such as transformers and other high-voltage equipment, most of which have long lead times for replacement (12 to 24 months) and are foreign-produced.

Further, energy industry groups have and continue to engage in exercises to plan for and ensure grid reliability. With implementation of FERC's electricity reliability authorities under the Energy Policy Act of 2005 (EPAct 2005), the Federal oversight role in electricity reliability is greatly enhanced.

Energy Sector owners and operators have well-developed protocols, organizations, and systems for ensuring the reliability of energy networks. The importance of sector assets, both physical and cyber, is affected by changing threats and continually changing consequences. Prioritization of assets and systems in the Energy Sector is dynamic—it changes constantly and goes on continuously. Static prioritization of assets could lead to critical decisionmaking based on outdated or erroneous asset information in efforts to direct scarce resources to those assets, systems, and networks that may be the most critical at any point in time. The public and private partners in the Energy Sector will continue its dialogue with DHS/DOE and other stakeholders to examine cross-sector needs and approaches to support DHS programs. DOE works with DHS to identify gaps in existing energy information and to identify publicly available databases or sources that could provide data to support DHS efforts to prioritize assets.

Some DHS, DOE, and other government programs need to allocate resources based on their prioritization (e.g., DHS's BZPP), SAVs and Comprehensive Reviews, as well as State and local initiatives. These programs supplement and support industry efforts. State and local efforts under the NIPP are also based on some measure of relative importance, risk consequence, and vulnerability of the critical infrastructure within their jurisdictions. This will require that State and local governments work with the sector owners and operators in their jurisdictions to understand the importance of critical facilities. In addition, stakeholders will need to address policy, regulatory, or other barriers to undertake needed measures and to allow for recovery of prudently incurred costs for those utilities subject to rate regulation. In addition DHS has provided funding to State and local entities based on risk assessments of critical infrastructure.

5. Develop and Implement Protective Programs and Resilience Strategies

Figure 5-1: Implement Protective Programs

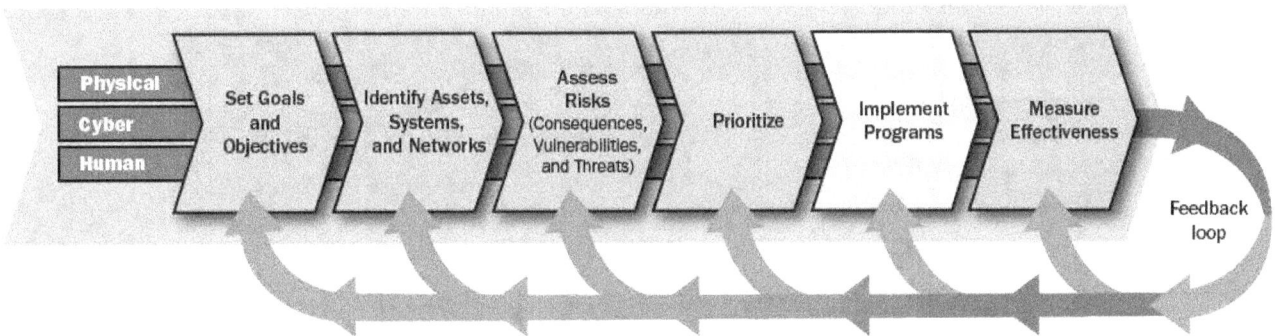

Figure 5-1: Implement Protective Programs

Continuous improvement to enhance protection of CIKR

5.1 Overview of Sector Protective Programs

With its Energy Sector partners, DOE will continue to evaluate existing protective programs and resilience strategies in order to further develop and support new programs that effectively reduce the vulnerability of critical energy assets. The overall strategy will focus on efforts that support the Energy Sector's goals of: 1) continuity of energy services and business through reliable information sharing, 2) effective physical and cyber security, and 3) coordinated response capabilities.

The cornerstone of the overall strategy is partnership with all key stakeholders in the public and private sectors. This approach will continue to take full advantage of the extensive experience and expertise of sector partners. It will also ensure that repercussions of planned activities are carefully considered. This section outlines the methods that partners in the Energy Sector use to assess, select, and implement cost-effective infrastructure protective programs. It also highlights some of the existing cooperative efforts within the sector.

5.2 Process for Evaluating, Prioritizing Needs, and Implementing Programs

The process for developing and implementing effective protective measures has three phases: 1) determining needs, 2) developing programs, and 3) finding long-term solutions (figure 5-2). The first phase builds on information sharing and partnerships to determine security needs. The second phase, program development and implementation, draws from effective practices already in use by industry and from national laboratory efforts. The last phase addresses R&D needs (which are discussed in chapter 7) and identifies long-term technological solutions for protecting and improving the resilience of physical assets, energy control systems, and related cyber systems. Some activities in different phases may proceed simultaneously, where feasible, to expedite improvements in CIP.

Throughout the process, DOE will continue to work with sector partners within the framework of the Energy SSP goals, which support the vision of a "robust, resilient energy infrastructure in which continuity of business and services is maintained through secure and reliable information sharing, effective risk management programs, coordinated response capabilities, and trusted relationships between public and private sector partners at all levels of industry and government." In the Energy Sector, this effort builds on ongoing voluntary industry cooperative actions that have been supplemented by regulatory regimes. DOE, as the SSA, works to encourage these voluntary industry efforts through the NIPP CIPAC partnership model.

Figure 5-2: Evaluating and Prioritizing Needs, and Implementing Programs

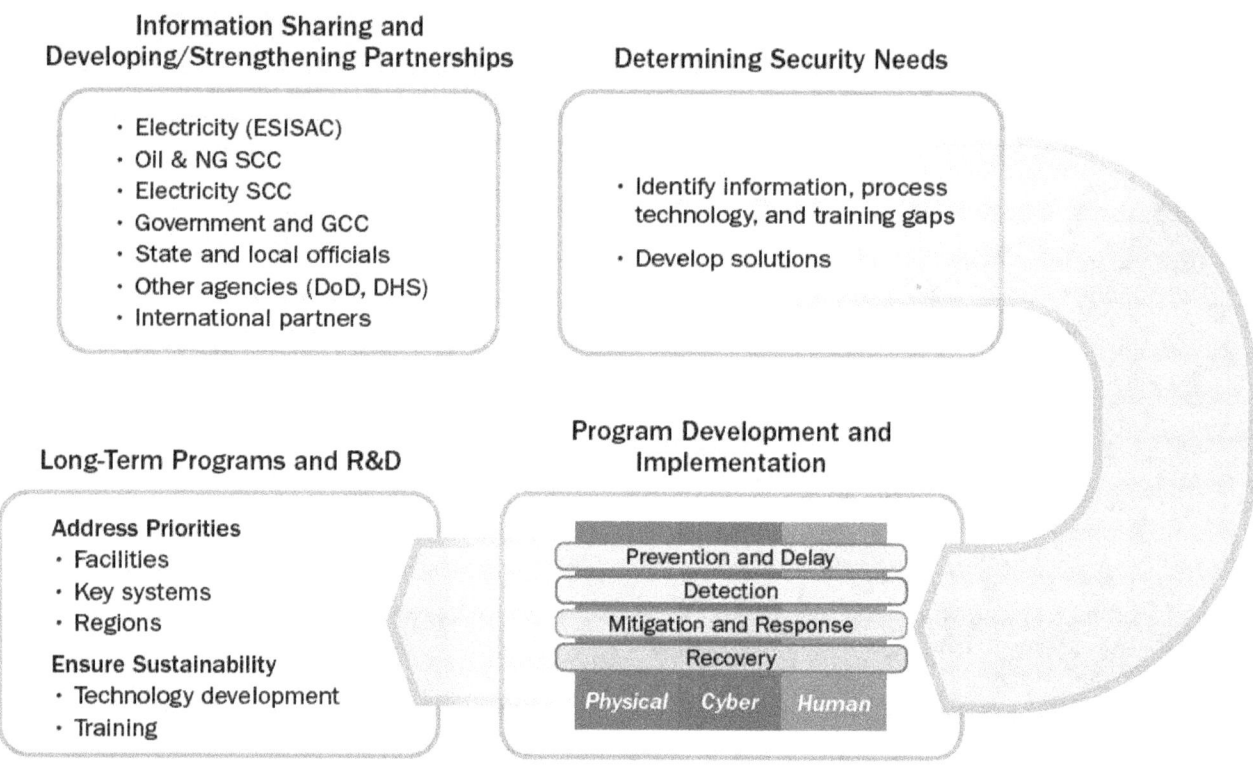

5.2.1 Enhanced Information Sharing and Needs Assessment

During the needs assessment phase, DOE continues to work closely with the industry and GCCs and its other partners to:

- Enhance current information-sharing practices and programs;

- Identify information gaps/needs;

- Augment current efforts to develop protection guidelines and programs;

- Develop an understanding of roles and responsibilities in strengthening protection of energy assets;

- Support owners and operators and their representatives in evaluating existing practices and guidelines for reducing physical and cyber vulnerabilities;

- Update and improve existing protective and resilience programs and methods as warranted;

- Conduct training and exercises that test and identify gaps in current approaches to security, preparedness, response, and energy assurance issues. Partner in that effort with industry representatives and Federal, State, and local officials. Recommend programs to address any identified gaps, and;

- Conduct site assistance visits to energy asset owners and operators.

5.2.2 Developing and Implementing Focused Programs

Public and private sector partners have been engaged in evaluating potential programs for specific assets or groups of assets. Industry expert groups have been working through their trade associations (e.g., NERC's CIPC, API's Security Committee) to discuss and examine approaches, effective practices, and best practices.

Establishing roles and responsibilities for the implementation of new resilience and protective measures and programs has presented—and will continue to present—both challenges and opportunities. DOE will continue to work with DHS and other agencies as well as industry owners and operators to examine policy and regulatory issues surrounding the establishment of such programs.

Furthermore, comprehensive programs that address the vulnerabilities of high-priority assets within the infrastructure have been and will continue to be implemented or enhanced, along with complementary training and exercise programs. Roles and responsibilities for developing, implementing, and maintaining resilience and protective programs are routinely revisited to clearly delineate among DOE, DHS, other Federal agencies (DOT and TSA, for example, regarding pipelines), sector asset owners, and State, local, and tribal officials.

5.3 Program Development and Sector Goals

Extensive programs are already in place to support and protect the Nation's energy resources and cyber assets. The 2009 Energy Sector Annual Report listed more than 120 programs underway in the sector. Review of these existing security programs – as well as development of new ones – is conducted within the framework of the sector's goals. These goals, as previously noted, can be grouped into four main categories: 1) information sharing and communication, 2) physical and cyber protection, 3) coordination and planning, and 4) public confidence. As the 2009 White House Cyberspace Policy Review warns, however, these programs are not adequate to combat the increasing threats that are facing the Nation's critical infrastructure.[48]

5.3.1 Information Sharing and Communication

Goal: Establish robust situational awareness within the Energy Sector through timely, reliable, and secure information exchange among trusted public and private sector partners.

Both industry and government need credible, timely, and actionable threat and hazard information to ensure that the most appropriate security investments, programs, and decisions are made to protect sector assets. Information on vulnerabilities, threats, and consequences is, by nature, sensitive. Unless both public and private sector partners trust that shared information will be strictly protected and used only for agreed-upon purposes, the costs of sharing sensitive information could be seen to outweigh the benefits, and the partnership could fail. Trusted relationships among decision makers who implement risk management programs provide the most effective foundation for coordinated response functions and effective information sharing programs.

---

[48] Cyberspace Policy Review: Assuring a Trusted and Resilient Information and Communications Infrastructure, 2009, **http://www.whitehouse.gov/assets/documents/ Cyberspace_Policy_Review_final.pdf**.

High on the list of challenges is the need to develop new methods—or to better explain existing methods—for collecting, protecting, and, as necessary, sharing sensitive data on the vulnerabilities of energy assets and the protective programs used to address them. These methods must be acceptable to all stakeholders. Industry is understandably cautious when providing information needed for vulnerability assessments, and when disclosing the results of assessments. Industry is equally cautious about providing specifics regarding ongoing and planned protective programs.

In response to such concerns, DOE has continued to work closely with industry, States, DHS, FERC, and other agencies to develop suitable information exchange policies, regulations, and procedures. The goal is to protect all industry information against inappropriate disclosure. DOE will also continue to work with the PCII Office within DHS's IP to apply provisions of the CII Act (and the implementing regulations of 6 CFR Part 29) to critical infrastructure information not customarily in the public domain and voluntarily submitted to DHS.

Figure 5-3: ESISAC Functions

- Receives incident data from private and public entities.
- Assists DOE, FERC, and DHS in analyzing event data to determine threat vulnerabilities and trends, as well as interdependencies with other critical infrastructures.
- Facilitates analysis of incident data and prepares information.
- Disseminates threat alerts, warnings, advisories, notices, and vulnerability assessments.
- Maintains a close operating liaison with other private and public government infrastructure information-sharing and analysis centers.
- Develops and maintains an awareness of private and government infrastructure interdependencies.
- Maintains a secure Internet site to facilitate messaging among participants.
- Participates in government infrastructure exercises.
- Conducts outreach.

5.3.1.1 Industry Programs

Both the Electricity and Oil and Natural Gas subsectors have made extensive efforts to share security information. In the electricity industry, NERC operates the ESISAC, which gathers, disseminates, and interprets security-related information (figure 5-3). It facilitates communication among electricity industry participants, Federal agencies, and other critical infrastructures, and helps electricity sector participants take protective action. In addition, a procedure for reporting suspected or real security incidents is in place along with a NERC standard that requires entities to report physical sabotage. The cyber standards adopted by the electricity industry also require reporting.

In the oil and natural gas industry, AGA, NPRA, API, and other oil and natural gas industry groups, have held numerous workshops and forums to discuss and share security information. The industry has also worked closely with DHS, DOT, and DOE to develop security guidelines and has continued to conduct regional planning studies to determine the impact of major pipeline system outages.

- Serves as a mechanism for gathering and disseminating private sector information as well as information from the Federal Government.
- Becomes a clearinghouse of information within and among various sectors of the energy industry.
- Becomes a repository of historical data to be used by its members.

5.3.1.2 Government Programs

In a joint effort, DHS has partnered with the Electricity and Oil and Natural Gas SCCs to develop HSIN, an Internet-based communications system[49] that enhances reporting and information sharing and allows industry participants to communicate securely with each other, with other industry sectors, and with government agencies (figure 5-4). The ONG SCC signed an MOU with DHS in May 2006 acknowledging that HSIN would serve as a primary information sharing tool within the ONG sector and with government.

DOE has also developed the ISERnet, a restricted-access communications network for key energy industry and State personnel to exchange information with DOE during energy emergencies. The site provides threat awareness and relevant security analyses and presentations.

Public Safety and Emergency Preparedness Canada (PSEPC) and DHS exchange government information via HSIN in order to coordinate preparedness across agencies. PSEPC and the Canadian Electricity Association regularly exchange information via voice and electronic media. PSEPC and NERC exchange information via ESISAC. In addition, DHS and PSEPC have the necessary mechanisms in place to facilitate sharing of electricity sector threat and vulnerability information between the Canadian and U.S. governments.

DHS/IP provides classified briefings and information for cleared members of the electricity and oil and natural gas industries to share classified information on the current threat situation, especially regarding impacts on the sector. This information is intended to enable attendees to assess risks facing the industry. Additionally, public and private sector partners are active participants in the NCSD working group, which discusses common cybersecurity issues affecting multiple CIKR sectors.

The EEAC system (discussed in chapter 1) is a cooperative effort among associations representing States, local governments, and DOE's OE/ISER. EEAC provides energy security information, including daily news summaries, emergency situation reports, lessons learned from other States, links to outage and curtailment information, and the ability to email messages to colleagues in other jurisdictions. In an energy supply disruption or emergency, DOE relies on these contacts to provide an up-to-date assessment of energy markets in the affected States. They serve as the link between the State, industry, and DOE.

5.3.2 Physical and Cyber Security

Goal: Use sound risk management principles to implement physical and cyber protective measures that enhance preparedness, security, and resilience.

DOE works with DHS and other partners throughout the sector to assure that current and potential threats are conveyed on a real-time basis to owners and operators. The need for increased and continuous vigilance is clear.

---

[49] HSIN is a secure, Internet-based system of integrated communication networks designed to facilitate information sharing between DHS and other Federal, State, county, local, tribal, and private sector commercial and other nongovernmental organizations involved in identifying and preventing terrorism, as well as in undertaking incident management activities.

The public and private partners in the Energy Sector have a long history of understanding and mitigating risk. The industry has responded to the increased need for enterprise-level security efforts and business continuity plans, and will continue to assess the security vulnerabilities of single-point assets such as refineries, storage terminals, and power plants, as well as networked features such as pipelines, transmission lines, and cyber systems.

Energy Sector asset owners and operators are working to address physical, cyber, and human risk and vulnerability issues. Assets identified as high priority are receiving additional attention. Investments to respond to these issues compete with other company investment requirements. DOE and DHS are working with Energy Sector partners to develop processes and methods for collection, protection, and use of data associated with government and industry resilience and protective programs.

5.3.2.1 Industry Resilience Programs

Today's transforming "information age" technology has intensified the importance of CIP, in which cybersecurity has become as critical as physical security to protecting energy CIKR. Owners and operators of the Energy Sector have rapidly responded to the increasing need for enterprise-level physical and cyber security efforts and business continuity plans. Voluntarily conducted vulnerability assessments have not only improved sector security but have also demonstrated industry commitment to a secure and resilient energy sector. Many asset owners and operators conduct self-assessments or contract with third parties to perform energy vulnerability assessments and implement protective programs at their facilities.

Electricity

NERC's CIP Reliability Standards (CIP-002-1 through CIP-009-1) were approved by FERC in January 2008. NERC's Version 2 CIP Reliability Standards (CIP-002-2 through CIP-009-2),[50] were approved by FERC in September 2009. The CIP Reliability Standards address multiple aspects of cyber asset protection, including:

* Data and information classification according to confidentiality;

* Identification and protection of cyber assets related to reliable operation of the bulk electric systems, and;

* Annual approval by senior management of the risk-based assessment methodology in addition to the list of critical cyber assets.

Oil and Natural Gas

The Oil and Natural Gas subsector has identified the following priorities:

* Assess security vulnerabilities at single-point assets such as refineries, storage terminals, and other buildings, as well as networked features such as pipelines and cyber systems, and;

* Work toward resilient, secure cyber networks and SCADA systems in order to detect and respond to cyber attacks.

AGA, INGAA, and APGA worked together to develop and release *Security Guidelines: Natural Gas Industry, Transmission and Distribution.* These guidelines provide an approach for vulnerability assessment, a critical facility definition, detection/deterrent methods, response and recovery guidance, cybersecurity information, and relevant operational standards. Based on the DHS Homeland Security Advisory System (HSAS), the guidelines incorporate a risk-based approach for natural gas companies to consider when identifying critical facilities and determining appropriate actions. TSA, along with PHMSA, has conducted onsite reviews based on these guidelines.

---

[50] http://www.nerc.com/page.php?cid=2 | 20.

5.3.2.2 Government Programs

PHMSA, in cooperation with energy and pipeline trade associations and State pipeline safety programs, has issued a security guidance information circular that defines critical pipeline facilities, identifies appropriate countermeasures for protecting them, and explains how PHMSA plans to verify that operators have taken appropriate action to implement satisfactory security procedures and plans.

Many State agencies, including public utility commissions, are responsible for administering Federal and State pipeline safety programs as established by 49 U.S.C. Chapter 601. Although pipeline security falls under the Transportation Systems SSP, pipelines are a key aspect of the energy infrastructure, and many States have safety regulatory responsibilities for them.

States and local government also have responsibilities for working with the private sector on the physical and cyber security of energy facilities. Public utility commissions are responsible for ensuring an adequate and reliable supply of electricity, natural gas, and in some cases, petroleum. They must address cost recovery of utility investments that protect and enhance the resilience of the energy infrastructure. Public utility commissions along with State energy offices also respond to energy supply disruptions and develop, maintain, and exercise contingency plans. Cybersecurity has been a concern of the commissions since the late 1990s, when questions arose about how reaching the year 2000 might affect computer and control systems (Y2K). Some States have also supported cybersecurity efforts by working with the InfraGard program.

State homeland security agencies are also responsible for ensuring that critical energy infrastructures are protected as part of State homeland security strategies. This effort includes working with DHS on comprehensive security reviews at key energy facilities and working with local governments to provide Buffer Zone Plans (BZPs) for protection of the perimeters of critical infrastructures. In some cases local governments also own and operate municipal electric utilities and have direct responsibility for undertaking risk and vulnerability assessments and implementing protective measures.

5.3.2.3 International Programs

The U.S. and Canadian governments have signed the Canada-United States CIP Framework for Cooperation, which recognizes their shared commitment to a secure and robust critical infrastructure. The framework includes energy, as well as transportation and other sector infrastructure, and is evidence of the mutual commitment by each country to work for the protection of shared critical infrastructure.

The United States and Mexico work together under a U.S.-Mexico Critical Infrastructure Framework for Cooperation. The CIP Bilateral Steering Committee oversees six working groups that implement the framework in the areas of energy, transportation, public health, telecommunications, food and agriculture, and water and dams.

Trilaterally, the Ad Hoc CIP Forum under the North American Energy Working Group (NAEWG) promotes a more fully integrated energy market in North America. NAEWG was established in 2001 by the U.S., Canadian, and Mexican energy departments.

In addition, the International Electricity Infrastructure Assurance Forum (IEIAF) is committed to sharing lessons learned and best practices regarding a wide variety of critical infrastructure threats and vulnerabilities. The group includes experts from Australia, Canada, New Zealand, the United Kingdom, and the United States.

5.3.3 Coordination and Planning

Goal: Conduct comprehensive emergency, disaster, and continuity of business planning, including training and exercises, to enhance reliability and emergency response.

Goal: Clearly define CIP roles and responsibilities among all Federal, State, local, and private sector partners.

Goal: Understand key sector interdependencies and cooperate with other sectors to address them, and incorporate that knowledge in planning and operations.

Coordination and cooperation are essential to planning and executing security programs and response and recovery activities. Security programs and emergency response planning are most effective when stakeholders clearly understand their respective roles and responsibilities and plan to integrate their independently executed roles to achieve a common set of infrastructure protection outcomes.

The Energy Sector depends on other sectors to help provide its services, and it provides energy services upon which numerous other sectors depend. Interdependencies also exist within the sector itself. Comprehensively understanding such interdependencies enables the sector to mitigate potential vulnerabilities and helps ensure the Nation's economy can continue to deliver goods and services during extraordinary events. DOE continues to work with sector partners to help identify program gaps and improve the effectiveness of sector infrastructure and resilience programs.

5.3.3.1 Coordination With Industry

In the Electricity subsector, collaboration between NERC and DOE allows for industry-government cooperation and coordination on CIP efforts in the physical and cyber security areas. NERC's CIPC coordinates several working groups and task forces that address specific issues related to NERC's security initiatives and protection of the electric system. CIPC is composed of industry experts in the areas of cybersecurity, physical security, and operational security. Both DOE and DHS participate in CIPC, allowing it to serve as a mechanism within the Electricity subsector for collaboration between industry and government. As such, CIPC is able to identify and close gaps in sector-wide efforts to meet the sector's goals. The CIPC Executive Committee also serves as the ESCC (section 1.3).

The oil and natural gas industries have also maintained longstanding partnerships with all levels of government in an effort to coordinate the infrastructure protection efforts associated with all hazards. Like the Electricity subsector, the Oil and Natural Gas subsector has worked with DOE, DHS, and DOT, to create its own security guidelines and security vulnerability assessment methodology. The ONG SCC and CIPAC provide additional mechanisms for the industry to improve collaboration among its members as well as with DOE, the Energy GCC, individual Federal agencies, and State government energy associations.

5.3.3.2 Coordination With Federal Government Agencies

DOE and the sector partners will continue to coordinate with other Federal agencies that have energy-related response and security responsibilities and energy-related programs. DOE will continue to support effective practices and partner, where practical, with these agencies in implementing protective programs. The responsibilities of various government agencies under the National Response Framework are an important element of intra-governmental cooperation during an energy emergency or other incident of national significance. During disruptions, DOE staff and emergency response support personnel work in conjunction with personnel from FEMA, other parts of DHS, EPA, DOT, State and local government, utilities, and others as they perform DOE's Emergency Support Function 12 (ESF-12) responsibilities. DOE has also partnered with FERC and several other Federal agencies, State regulators, and industry to assess the implications of a loss of natural gas supply to certain regions of the Nation.

5.3.3.3 Coordination With States and Localities

State and local governments have a unique role in energy assurance because they represent the front lines of protection and the face of public services to citizens during an emergency. As the SSA for the energy infrastructure, DOE has engaged State and local energy leaders, and the organizations that represent them, in an effort to identify their energy assurance needs and implement programs directed at improving the reliability and safety of their energy infrastructure.

Figure 5-5: DOE ARRA

DOE ARRA State and Local Energy Assurance Planning Initiative

To facilitate State and local energy assurance planning activities, DOE's OE/ISER is providing guidance, support, and training to recipients of funds under the ARRA. The Energy Assurance Planning Initiative for State and local (city) governments is a major element of DOE's responsibly to lead and develop ways to improve the Nation's Energy Sector resilience. The overall goal of the three-year program (2009-2012) is to hone a standardized, comprehensive energy assurance and resilience approach that will benefit localities, States, and the Nation. The purpose of this implementation strategy is to provide a multi-phased, flexible, and cost-effective master work plan and a schedule of tasks and activities to meet this goal.

The ARRA directly supports and expands DOE efforts to work in collaboration with States and localities as well as their energy providers. This collaboration will strengthen planning and overall capability to prevent, mitigate, respond to, and facilitate expedited recovery from energy disruptions. State and local government agencies participating in the ARRA Energy Assurance Planning Initiative have largely similar objectives:

- Create and save jobs to develop and implement effective energy assurance and resilience plans.
- Enhance in-house expertise on infrastructure interdependencies and related vulnerabilities, including: cybersecurity, energy supply systems, energy data analysis, communications, and areas for improvement to lessen the economic and health and safety impacts of energy disruptions.
- Develop and initiate a process or mechanism for tracking the duration, response, and restoration and recovery time of energy supply disruptions.
- Develop new plans, or refine existing ones, and incorporate them into a broader emergency management effort to enhance the resilience and protection of critical energy infrastructure. Revise current policies, procedures, and practices to reflect the Energy Assurance Plans.
- Conduct energy emergency exercises to evaluate the effectiveness of the Energy Assurance Plans.
- Build organizational relationships and identify responsibilities within local and State government, the private sector, and the region that support public/private partnerships.
- Integrate new energy portfolios (e.g., renewables, biofuels) and new applications, such as Smart Grid technology, into energy assurance and emergency preparedness plans.

Energy reliability, assurance, and resilience planning; technology development; and infrastructure improvements are often fragmented, stove-piped, uncoordinated, and stymied for a variety of reasons at the State and local levels. In many States and local jurisdictions, responsibility for energy assurance issues falls under different agencies and authorities including State energy offices, public utility commissions, emergency management, homeland security, and economic planning agencies, among others. Interaction between State and local (city) officials on energy assurance issues or among local jurisdictions—even when in the same region or sharing the same energy providers—varies across the Nation and is typically less well-coordinated than needed.

In addition, there is insufficient understanding of energy-associated infrastructure interdependencies that can go beyond local jurisdiction and State boundaries. There is also insufficient recognition of the need for a regional integrated energy assurance strategy that takes into account supply (traditional energy sources and renewables), distribution (electricity transmission and pipelines, Smart Grid investment), energy efficiency, security, climate change, and in particular, disaster resilience needs. The Energy Assurance Planning Initiative is intended to address the shortfalls of limited State and local government staff, resources, and expertise by developing effective plans and mitigation measures that will enhance preparedness and management of all-hazards energy emergencies.

NASEO, in collaboration with NARUC, has produced Energy Assurance Guidelines (**www.naseo.org/eaguidelines**) that outline States' overall role in energy assurance. This role includes operating within the Federal ESF structure, organizing and building response mechanisms, coordinating with stakeholders, planning response strategies, profiling energy use and vulnerability, and identifying fuel-related response measures. NARUC and NASEO have worked with DOE to conduct multi-State and regional exercises and training sessions on energy emergency preparedness, response, and key CIP issues. NASEO, with DOE support, has also provided direct technical assistance to States to update their energy assurance plans. These efforts will continue and expand under the Energy Assurance Planning Grants provided to States and local (city) governments under the funding provided by the ARRA.

DOE will continue to work with State and local governments. Together, they will identify gaps in meeting sector goals, improve existing State-focused programs, and implement new programs to eliminate identified vulnerabilities. The State, Local, Tribal, and Territorial (SLTT) GCC, formed in 2007, consists of partners from all CIKR sectors and is critical in NIPP implementation. Two SLTT GCC representatives with energy backgrounds have been appointed to work with the Energy GCC. Due to State responsibilities for public utilities that provide a direct service to their citizens, States are particularly concerned with programs related the sharing of information with other critical sectors (see figure 5-6). Public utility commissions also support emergency management and response activities during events that affect utility facilities, systems, and services.

Figure 5-6: Public Utility Commissions

Public utility commissions provide an example of a State entity with responsibility for electricity, gas, and telecommunications infrastructure and, in some cases, water, wastewater/sewage, and certain aspects of transportation. As such, public utility commissions are uniquely positioned to deal with the recovery of investments made for CIP in these areas. Furthermore, the commissions historically have been concerned with the adequacy and reliability of these services, and have facilitated investments made by these industries to ensure they are resilient and reliable.

For example, public utility commissions work together to address issues of mutual concern based on the interdependencies among the water, telecommunications, and energy infrastructure (in the context of preparedness for, and response to, events impacting critical infrastructure) by:

· Creating networks among utility regulators and other Federal, State, local, and private sector entities to address cross-sector issues.

· Exploring and recommending solutions for information disclosure issues (especially protecting sensitive security information from public disclosure while ensuring that all critical stakeholders have access to essential information).

· Exploring and recommending solutions to cost-recovery issues associated with key water, gas, telecommunications, and energy infrastructure.

· Identifying and prioritizing issues, researching best practices, and disseminating information to Federal and State partners and affiliates.

Additional examples of cooperative programs with the States are included in table 5-1.

Figure 5-7: Southeastern Electric Exchange Mutual Assistance Group

The Southeastern Electric Exchange has had a formal working mutual aid group since the 1950s. The group has established written guidelines for requesting and providing emergency assistance that are continuously improved and refined. The Edison Electric Institute (EEI) has created the "Joint Mobilization" process which includes establishing a procedure for initiating "Mutual Assistance Conference Calls." This procedure allows a company in need of assistance to contact all members with one phone call. After each call, all members receive summary notes and a "Resource Summary Sheet," which details the resources needed and available, including companies and contract personnel. Most commonly requested and identified resources include distribution linemen, transmission linemen, vegetation management personnel, and damage assessment personnel.

At least five other mutual assistance groups have adopted conference call procedures similar to those of the Southeastern Electric Exchange.

5.3.3.4 Regional Coordination

Sector partners need to coordinate on the national level to ensure synergy of efforts and efficiencies. Regional coordination, however, is even more important, especially regarding response to actual events. DHS established RCCC to encourage regional cooperation and stimulate the sharing of best and most effective approaches. States and local governments are also encouraged to coordinate their planning under the ARRA Energy Assurance Planning Grants and to test these plans as part of the intra- and inter-State exercises provided for under this initiative. In the Electricity subsector, cooperation between utilities on a regional basis has been taking place for many years. There are eight Regional Mutual Assistance Groups at present: Great Lakes, Mid-Atlantic, Midwest, New York, Southeastern Electric Exchange, Texas, Western Region, and Wisconsin. Figure 5-7 provides an example of how such regional cooperation can work.

Similarly, the Pacific Northwest Economic Region (PNWER) provides an example of regional coordination between public and private partnerships. The organization includes legislators, State governments, and businesses in five States and three Canadian provinces. PNWER sponsors interdependency exercises and has developed an action plan outlining several physical and cyber CIKR regional protection projects. PNWER also participates in the Northwest Warning, Alert, Response Network (NW-WARN), a DHS pilot project. PNWER will also provide training opportunities on energy assurance planning and resilience for legislators through their Energy Horizon Legislative Institute. This effort is being coordinated with NCSL.

5.3.3.5 International Coordination

The U.S. Energy Sector relies on energy and technology imported from other countries. Therefore, it is critical that the United States work closely with these countries to reduce physical and cyber vulnerabilities within their own energy sectors, as these vulnerabilities could affect the U.S. energy infrastructure. The Cyberspace Policy Review highlighted the need to develop a U.S. government position for an international cybersecurity policy framework and to strengthen international partnerships to create initiatives that would address cybersecurity activities.[51] DOE, in conjunction with DHS, DOS, DOC, and other Federal agencies, cooperates in bilateral and multilateral forums with other countries.

The United States and Canada have a well-established history of collaboration and cooperation on electricity reliability, primarily through NERC. EPAct 2005 requires implementation of mandatory electricity reliability standards in the United States. These

---

[51] Cyberspace Policy Review: Assuring a Trusted and Resilient Information and Communications Infrastructure, 2009, **http://www.whitehouse.gov/assets/documents/Cyberspace_Policy_Review_final.pdf**.

reliability standards have been adopted in several Canadian provinces. Pipeline interconnections between the United States and Canada and between the United States and Mexico move considerable volumes of oil and gas between the countries. This also requires coordination to ensure that protective measures across borders provide adequate risk reduction across the full length of these systems.

5.3.4 Public Confidence

Goal: Strengthen partner and public confidence in the sector's ability to manage risk and implement effective security, reliability, and recovery efforts.

Industry and government officials will work together to communicate to Congress, regulators, and the general public that the industry's public-private partnership is working effectively to ensure sector security. Agencies and industry associations have publicized their efforts. DOE will continue to work through the SCC and GCC members to support additional ways to enhance public confidence, including education and communication programs.

Table 5-1: Key Risk Mitigation Activities

Sector Goal from Energy SSP	Risk Mitigation Activity Descriptions	Output Data	Progress
Information Sharing and Communications	Promote security, infrastructure integrity, and reliability of energy systems. Convene via meetings, conferences, tabletop exercises, forums, workshops, and training courses to facilitate security information exchange. Provide a national Web-based platform to share homeland security information with sector partners. Examples include: · NERC ESISAC · AGA Natural Gas Security Committee · APPA Security Committee and Listserver · EEI IT Working Group, Security Committee · EEI Business Continuity Task Force and Working Group · NPRA Security Committee · NGA Center for Best Practices' Energy Assurance Briefings and Guidance · ILTA Security Working Group · API Security Committee · DHS-IP HSIN	· API holds security committee meetings three times per year and IT security forums quarterly · NPRA holds several workshops, TTXs, and conferences to share effective security practices	Efforts expanded by the creation of an Energy Emergency Working Group under API which includes some 38 oil and natural gas and chemical companies. Security committees continue to be very active, and each meets several times a year.

Sector Goal from Energy SSP	Risk Mitigation Activity Descriptions	Output Data	Progress
Physical Security	Develop contingency plans in the event of a threat. Schedule visits to and perform physical vulnerability assessments of select energy facilities. Target Energy Sector sites housing specified minimum levels of designated chemicals. Enhance security efforts. Examples include: · NERC Influenza Pandemic Planning, Preparation, and Response Reference Guide · Natural Gas Pipeline Regional Disruption Project · USCG Area Maritime Security Committees · USCG Port Security Inspections · National Guard Bureau's HLD-eCAM · DOE-developed Power Plant and Refinery Annexes · DHS-IP CFATS	· DOE Reliability, Survivability, and Resiliency efforts initially targeted refineries; development of an Internet-based approach continues. · USCG Area Maritime Security Committees enhance security efforts in about 50 major ports by helping the port captains coordinate planning, information sharing, and other necessary activities. · In April 2007, there were six CIP-Mission Assurance pilot teams with the National Guard Bureau.	Electricity guidelines and standards through NERC are being implemented; considerable progress has been made; Transportation Work Identification Credential (TWIC) program is making progress in implementation.
Cybersecurity	Define protocol for securing systems against possible cybersecurity attacks and provide a model for proactive industry actions to improve infrastructure security. Also identify potential vulnerabilities and help improve protection of SCADA networks and advise and assist boards of directors on cybersecurity and cyber terrorism Examples include: · AGA Cryptographic Protection of SCADA Communication · API Pipeline SCADA Security Standard (API Standard 1164) · DOE National SCADA Test Bed Program · DOE Roadmap · DOE 21 Steps to Improve the Cyber Security of SCADA Networks · NPRA Cyber Security Subcommittee · NERC Cyber Security Standards	· SCADA R&D Roadmap is broadly disseminated in the Energy Sector and has been a model for other sectors. NERC has assessed the possible impact of one identified SCADA vulnerability. · Nine cyber-related guidelines and standards are in the process of being implemented by NERC. Standards are backed by possible penalties and reporting requirements.	· Warnings from DHS-NCSD and SERT disseminated through HSIN and the ESISAC; cyber-focused high-level intelligence briefing held in January 2009 for senior-level electricity officials. · Mandatory cyber standards have been implemented in the Electricity subsector and general principles of cyber protection are broadly accepted in the Oil and Natural Gas subsector.

Sector Goal from Energy SSP	Risk Mitigation Activity Descriptions	Output Data	Progress
Physical and CyberSecurity	Analyze current security risks and provide information to support effective risk reduction decisions. Provide funding for programs that reduce losses from future disasters or help prevent catastrophes. Also provide reporting and storing of incident information. Examples include: • BPA RAM-TSM • FEMA Federal Hazard Mitigation Program • TSA Pipeline Corporate Security Review • IFIP partners and USACE Incident Reporting System program	DHS' PSA program and DOE ESF staff have increased coordination with all ten FEMA regions. DOE has developed the ESF-12 Operations Manual and built and tested the Energy Response Center for use during energy emergencies.	Federal programs at the FEMA regional level have been expanded by DOE through ESF-12 training and establishment of regional responsibility.
Planning	Implement agreements that require partici-pants to maintain transformers for possible sharing in the event of a terrorist act. Provide guidance on strategy for needed preparedness. Examples include: • EEI (and a large group of electric utilities) Spare Transformer Sharing Agreement • TISP Guide for an Action Plan to Develop Regional Disaster Resilience • Electricity industry's voluntarily sharing crews during energy emergency	• EEI (and a large group of electric utilities) Spare Transformer Sharing Agreement includes more than 40 trans-mission-facility owners who have developed and signed a spare transformer agreement by which they maintain a specified number of high-voltage spare transform-ers and provide them if an act of terrorism occurs. • TSIP Guide for an Action Plan was developed by a TISP task force of more than 100 practitioners, policymakers, and technical and scientific experts from across the Nation.	Voluntary cooperation has been enhanced after hurri-canes in 2005 on both the national and regional levels. Electric utility agreements to support restoration are well established. The benefits are well recognized by the industry. Restoration support in natural gas is being developed as a result of utilization following Hurricane Katrina and flooding in New Orleans.
Planning	Produce a more effective, coordinated, global response to terrorism involving weapons of mass destruction (WMD) –involves senior Federal, State, and local officials. Examples include: • DHS Grant Programs Directorate National Level Exercise • FEMA Protection and National Preparedness, National Exercise Division	A DOE international program has been developed to assist key energy-producing allies in their efforts to protect energy assets. Work is proceeding in this area.	Cooperation with DOS and DoD is well established and efforts are underway to support energy infrastructure expertise abroad.

Sector Goal from Energy SSP	Risk Mitigation Activity Descriptions	Output Data	Progress
Coordination	Coordinate to maintain the ability of member-utilities to manage risk and implement effective security, system reliability, and recovery efforts as needed to ensure public confidence. Include coordination among all levels of government (Federal, State, local, and tribal) as well as control-system owners, operators, and vendors to improve control-system security within and across all CIKR sectors. Examples include: · NWPP and WECC Reliability and Coordination Programs · DHS-NCSD Control Systems Security Initiative	N/A	Several key sectors, including the Energy, Defense Industrial Base, Water, Banking and Finance, Agriculture and Food, Dams, and Chemical Sectors, discuss issues and approaches that impact multiple sectors.
Public Confidence	Recognize APPA member utilities that meet stringent guidelines and levels of attainment in the areas of reliability, safety, cybersecurity, mutual aid, disaster management, R&D, and system improvement. Examples include: · APPA RP3 Program, which requires municipal utilities to show they are addressing areas of DOE/DHS concern. Areas such as disaster management and preparedness (including NIMS), NERC standards and registration, cyber and physical security planning, and mutual aid are all part of the graded application. · DOE Energy Sector Modeling and Analysis through five national laboratories is broadly shared with sector partners. · DOE Situation Reports are placed on the DOE homepage during energy emergencies.	As of April 2008, 132 APPA members have earned their RP3, representing 26 percent of customers. DOE responds to FEMA emergency requests as ESF-12 lead and assists in restoration and recovery in energy-related emergencies. Training of ESF-12 responders now in its 4th year, has created a cadre of trained Energy Sector specialists for possible deployment when necessary.	Increasing cooperation between Federal agencies, State and local governments, and private sector owners and operators is recognized, with utilities increasing use of Web sites to inform customers and the media during energy-related emergencies.

5.4 Program Performance, Gaps, and Challenges

Table 5.2 lists some of the recommendations from energy industry symposia held to discuss lessons learned. Many of the industry recommendations present challenges to be addressed or indicate a need for education on response procedures and legal restrictions. Chapter 6 addresses metrics that may be used to evaluate program performance.

Table 5-2: Energy Sector Gaps and Recommendations

Transportation and Access to Disaster Areas
· Develop personnel and vehicle identification to control access to disaster areas to facilitate restoration efforts. · Provide assistance for travel within and to and from disaster areas in clearing roads and helping local public safety officials manage traffic flow. · Facilitate the availability of fuel supplies to be used for restoration equipment and crew transportation.

Health and Safety of Utility Crews Deployed in Disaster Areas
· Facilitate the health and safety of utility crews in disaster areas. · Educate responding government agencies on the need to facilitate delivery of supplies and equipment needed by crews and other critical infrastructure workers. · Advise companies of requirements for inoculations and other preventive health care considerations before crews are sent to disaster areas.

Communications
· Collect and disseminate appropriate outage and restoration information via existing emergency communication channels such as NERC, State emergency agencies, DOE 417 reports, or trade associations, as well as the EEAC and the ISERnet secure Web sites. · Coordinate and prioritize the restoration process between government and energy companies. · Provide priority status on cellular and satellite communication systems to all key sector partners.

Pre-Event Coordination
· Develop mutual contact information for key personnel and protocols for utilizing it. · Plan and coordinate disaster-planning drills on State and regional bases. · Compile a document of all State and Federal government programs and plans that could help companies and crews responding to disasters.

Two 2009 National Infrastructure Advisory Committee reports provided recommendations for dealing with disasters and related interdependencies, and for improving critical infrastructure resilience.[52] A number of these recommendations address the gaps identified in the 2007 Energy SSP and are shown in table 5-3.

Table 5-3: NIAC Recommendations

Categories	Recommendations
Fortify government policy framework	· Revise the current government policy guidance to incorporate resilience goals into a national policy.
Clarify roles and responsibilities of critical infrastructure partners	· Establish national and sector goals for resilience as part of the CIPAC and NIPP planning process. · Utilizing the CIPAC and sector partnership frameworks, engage CIKR owners and operators to form a common understanding of national resilience goals. · Support development of voluntary metrics.

---

[52] The National Infrastructure Advisory Council (NIAC), Critical Infrastructure Resilience Final Report, September 8, 2009, http://www.dhs.gov/xlibrary/assets/niac/ niac_critical_infrastructure_resilience.pdf (accessed July 23, 2010); NIAC, Framework for Dealing with Disasters and Related Interdependencies Final Report, July 14, 2009, http://www.dhs.gov/xlibrary/assets/niac/niac_framework_dealing_with_disasters.pdf (accessed July 23, 2010).

Categories	Recommendations
Strengthen and leverage public-private partnership	• Present collaboration on resilience as a true partnership of equals. • Foster rebuilding and reconstituting of the Nation's infrastructure to enhance efficiency and resilience. (Example: Smart Grid development). • Enable effective information sharing by becoming a neutral catalyst to facilitate partnerships between competitors and provide protection of information through the exemption to the Federal Advisory Committee Act.
Work with CIKR owners and operators	• Engage CIKR owners and operators in cross-sector emergency planning exercises. • Partner with CIKR owners to identify possible approaches to promote the adoption of more resilient practices.
Address statutory, regulatory, and policy impediments	• Consider possible approaches for granting temporary waivers of certain regulations to speed recovery efforts during emergencies.
Foster public-private cooperation and communication	• Develop commonly-applicable protocols for credentialing CIKR workers and granting them access to disaster areas during emergencies. • Collaborate with and improve preparedness exercises at all levels, including private sector CIKR owners and operators. • Elevate water services to its own ESF to achieve higher prioritization of water system during emergency response. Electricity (for pumping stations) and chemicals for water treatment (to meet potability requirements) are particularly dependent on water services.
Address possible uses of Federal statutory authorities	• Robert T. Stafford Disaster Relief and Emergency Assistance Act • Defense Production Act of 1950 2009 Amendments

While progress has been made in a number of areas, additional work is needed to improve sector resilience, restoration, and recovery. Electricity industry experts meeting at a workshop to discuss HILF events have identified suggestions in several areas.

In the area of prevention, recommendations include:

• Enhancing threat profile analysis (domestic and overseas)

• Promoting wider dissemination of analytical products

• Institutionalizing suspicious activities reporting

• Sharing real time information

• Developing a comprehensive insider threat approach

In the area of vulnerability reduction, recommendations include:

• Encouraging more comprehensive analysis and modeling, including dependencies/interdependencies, single points of failure, and system level vulnerabilities;

• Enhancing system robustness and resilience;

• Examining approaches to relieve potential component, spares, and supply chain stress;

• Building in design security and remote device physical security, and;

• Encouraging distributed energy generation and analysis of its potential impacts and implications.

In the area of emergency response, recommendations include:

• Further developing enhanced situational awareness/monitoring

• Examining Energy Sector surge capacity issues (equipment and people)

• Encouraging inter-utility agreements, MOUs, and EMACs

• Promoting public preparedness and risk communication

6. Measure Effectiveness

Figure 6-1: Measure Effectiveness

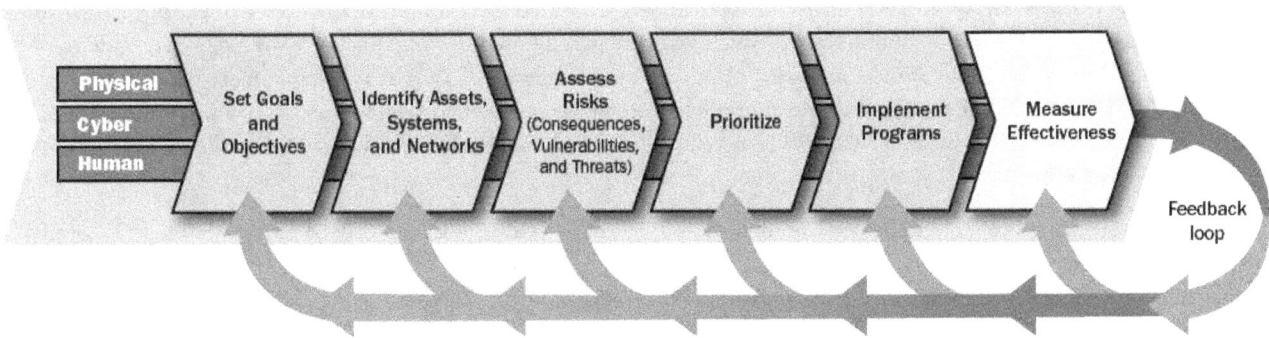

Continuous improvement to enhance protection of CIKR

DOE continues to work with sector partners to measure progress toward achieving the critical infrastructure protection goals outlined in chapter 1. An effective performance measurement system identifies appropriate metrics for measuring progress, collects relevant data on each metric, and uses that data to improve performance and provide accountability. DOE and sector partners continue the process of identifying metrics that are specific to the sector to supplement the DHS-developed metrics that are common across all CIKR sectors. Once metrics have been identified and agreed upon, initial assessments will be conducted to provide baseline information on each metric.

The sector recognizes that the measurement process itself can expose sensitive information about the vulnerability and protective capability of the energy infrastructure. DOE and sector partners are working with the PCII Program Office within DHS IP to apply the provisions of the CII Act, and the implementing regulations contained in 6 CFR Part 29, to critical infrastructure information that is not customarily in the public domain and is voluntarily submitted to DHS or DOE. DOE has had considerable experience in protecting sensitive energy-related critical infrastructure information, and will use this information only for national infrastructure protection purposes.

6.1 Key Risk Mitigation Activities

Sector partners continue to perform the activities deemed necessary to maintain a robust, resilient energy infrastructure. However, successful completion of these actions often depends on the availability of public and private resources.

DOE, as the SSA for energy, works with the Energy SCCs and Energy GCC to execute its responsibilities. Efforts are built on existing work in government agencies as well as private sector partners.

Key risk mitigation activities are identified in the Energy Sector Annual Report. These are shown in table 5-1. More than 125 activities in the Energy Sector have been identified which support the SSP goals. The table shows the key categories of activity in support of these goals and provides some examples of programs or outcomes in each area. DOE is working with sector partners to identify and quantify outcomes.

6.2 CIKR Performance Measurement

6.2.1 Metrics

6.2.1.1 Energy CIP Metrics

Metrics are a set of descriptive, process, and outcome indicators that measure progress made by individual sectors in the implementation of the NIPP. As the SSA, DOE is developing Energy CIP metrics in conjunction with sector partners. This work is conducted through the Metrics Working Group, which was established under the Joint Energy Working Group, authorized by the CIPAC. Along with the Energy SCCs, Energy GCC, TSA, and the Chemical SSA, DOE is working to identify physical, cybersecurity, reliability, and resilience metrics appropriate and relevant to the various energy subsectors. Once a more complete set of metrics has been agreed upon, methods will also be developed to collect and report data in a way that protects responses from inappropriate disclosure.

The CIP metrics, once approved, will be periodically reviewed by the SCCs and GCC, and may be modified to meet the evolving challenges facing the sector. Over time, some qualitative measures will be replaced with quantitative indicators as well as output and outcome metrics.[53] These qualitative measures and sector-specific metrics will be supplemented with examples of how sector performance is measured.

Process for Measuring Effectiveness

Sector partners have made considerable progress in the development of performance metrics since the release of the 2007 Energy SSP. This step is critical in the overall NIPP risk management framework. The metrics will allow DHS, DOE, and sector partners to objectively and quantitatively assess the sector's progress toward meeting its CIP goals and objectives. To facilitate the development of sector-specific metrics, the CIPAC Joint Energy Metrics Working Group was formed in late 2007. The group enables members of the Electricity and Oil and Natural Gas subsectors to collaborate in the metrics development process. It also provides feedback to the DHS Metrics Working Group. In addition, some members of the Joint Energy Metrics Working Group are working with the Chemical Sector and TSA Pipeline Working Group to ensure consistency across their metrics.

Electricity Subsector Metrics

Development of Electricity subsector performance metrics is well underway. DOE, NERC, and FERC are collaborating to develop metrics appropriate for reporting progress and tracking performance. NERC reliability standards and the resulting compliance audit data will be instrumental in developing these metrics. Although the reliability standards are in different stages of implementation, preliminary reporting has started under NERC guidance. The level of compliance and non-compliance, including the number and severity of violations, as well as any subsequent remediation activities, will serve as indicators of the Electricity subsector's progress.

---

[53] Output metrics measure whether specific activities were performed as planned to track progression of a task or report on the output of a process (such as inventorying assets). Outcome metrics track progress toward a strategic goal by the beneficial results rather than by the level of activity. See the NIPP, p. 47.

Currently, the Oil and Natural Gas subsector is developing its own performance metrics. In summer 2008, the Oil and Natural Gas SCC, Energy GCC, and DHS sponsored a workshop focusing on CIKR protection and resilience metrics for the Oil and Natural Gas subsector. The workshop, co-chaired by the AGA and DOE, identified five guiding principles for the development of Oil and Natural Gas subsector performance metrics:

1. Recognize the sheer diversity of the oil and natural gas industry.

2. Keep it simple.

3. A few applicable metrics are better than many inappropriate metrics.

4. Recognize that the inherent variability of operations drives the need for risk-based evaluations.

5. Metrics must be aligned cross-sector and cross-governmental agency.

Subsequent to the workshop, members of the Oil and Natural Gas subsector have begun to work with the Chemical Sector voluntary program. Alignment between these two groups is particularly important because many oil and natural gas companies and assets are related to the Chemical Sector. The subsector has also drafted a cybersecurity performance metrics questionnaire consistent with that of the PCIS Cyber Metrics Working Group, which was developed in conjunction with DHS NCSD.

6.2.2 Information Collection and Verification

DOE and its sector partners are working to identify sources of information and methods for collecting and sharing data on sector CIP metrics once they are identified.

6.2.3 Reporting

Sector metrics data will be reported annually to DHS by DOE. All data will be reported at a summary level and will be suppressed if they could reveal information about an individual company or asset.

6.3 Using Metrics for Continuous Improvement

Data on the sector-specific and other metrics will be examined to determine whether additional actions could be taken that might improve the security and resilience of the sector. For example, if only a small portion of the sector is participating in HSIN, then sector partners could be asked why they are not involved. Appropriate corrective actions would depend on the reasons for not participating, but may range from disseminating additional information about the benefits of participating to notifying DHS of particular problems with the network. Both the Oil and Natural Gas and Electricity subsector partners are currently working with DHS to identify new or improved uses for the HSIN information sharing platform.

There are numerous challenges in using data for continuous improvement. First, data collection is costly and time-consuming. Second, sector partners participate on a voluntary basis. Creative approaches may be needed to encourage participation. Third, some of the data that could be collected are sensitive. Some partners may be unwilling or unable to provide some types of information. Despite these challenges, DOE will work with sector partners to implement continuous improvement principles.

7. CIKR Protection R&D

7.1 Overview of Sector R&D

R&D is a key source of innovation and productivity for the Energy Sector. The equipment and systems used to extract, refine, transport, generate, and deliver energy are among the most technologically sophisticated of any economic sector. The high levels of reliability and productivity achieved by our Nation's Energy Sector are largely a result of significant private and public capital investments made in new physical and cyber technologies.

Energy owners and operators have worked with government, national laboratories, universities, industry organizations, and other key stakeholders to drive technological innovation throughout the sector.

Improved infrastructure security and resilience have become increasingly significant objectives of Energy Sector stakeholders' comprehensive technology R&D portfolio, as functionality and productivity are now coupled more closely with protective measures. The Energy Sector is composed of many different elements, each associated with different types of assets, business conditions, and risk profiles that define their distinctive and diverse R&D priorities. Companies work closely with their vendors, technology developers, customers, and research institutions to plan and manage R&D activities to meet their particular operating and security needs.

The commitment of sector owners and operators to reliable energy services and a robust, resilient infrastructure depends on effective physical and cyber security protection. In the near term, many companies will enhance their protective posture by adopting existing technologies, effective practices, and low-cost retrofits. The current energy infrastructure represents a massive capital investment that cannot be easily replaced even if new technologies become available. As energy companies and utilities expand their physical plants and replace older capital stock, new technologies that incorporate enhanced security features may be adopted.

Federal R&D investments exist in many government agencies and are coordinated with those of the private sector as part of an effective and robust national R&D strategy. DOE works with DHS and other funding agencies to highlight sector R&D needs and help identify priorities in cooperation with sector partners. In particular, Federal R&D seeks to fill gaps and stimulate private investment, particularly where market forces alone are insufficient to attract adequate private R&D funding. Leveraging public and private R&D investment in collaborative projects of mutual benefit is a central principle in the Federal energy R&D strategy for CIP.

As the lead agency for energy, DOE has a long history of collaborating with sector partners to develop new technologies. Since September 11, 2001, DOE, DHS, and other Federal agencies have collaborated on new technologies that will improve protection of energy assets. Sector partners and the Federal Government are using the sector partnership model to enhance this collaboration.

7.2 Energy Sector R&D

Sector stakeholders have become increasingly concerned about the security of the energy infrastructure. Since the 1990s, various groups such as the President's Commission on Critical Infrastructure Protection, NERC, and the National Petroleum Council have conducted numerous studies on the vulnerability and reliability of the Nation's energy infrastructure. Since September 11, 2001, additional studies, such as those conducted by the National Research Council[54] and RAND Corporation,[55] have examined the vulnerabilities and R&D needs of the sector in the new threat environment. In total, more than 100 studies of the energy infrastructure have been completed.

While these studies contain a variety of R&D recommendations, many were compiled by the research communities with little input from the private sector. The energy industry has a keen understanding of system operations and the potential consequences of critical failures, and shares responsibility for advancing R&D to make energy assets more secure. Government has also become increasingly aware of the need to stimulate security improvements in a competitive energy market that may inhibit private investment in security R&D. Consequently, industry and government are now actively working together to coordinate technology development through R&D roadmaps, government program reviews, and professional conferences and workshops to leverage limited resources for maximum gain.

7.2.1 Cybersecurity R&D Requirements

In 2005, DOE and DHS, in collaboration with Natural Resources Canada, facilitated an industry-led effort to define the top R&D needs for improving the cybersecurity of the North American energy infrastructure. This effort involved industry leaders from the electricity, oil, natural gas, and telecommunications sectors, as well as representatives from a broad cross-section of control system experts, commercial system vendors, industry associations, universities, national laboratories, and government agencies. This culminated in the January 2006 publication of the *Roadmap to Secure Control Systems in the Energy Sector*[56] (Control Systems Roadmap), which identifies concrete steps to secure control systems in the electricity, oil, and natural gas infrastructures through 2016. The Control Systems Roadmap established four main cybersecurity goals and addressed the full spectrum of cybersecurity priorities in the sector, including effective practices, standards, tools, information sharing, and training. Table 7-1 highlights the resulting milestones that the sector must achieve to accomplish the 10-year vision for control systems.

To meet the milestones, DOE's National SCADA Test Bed (NSTB) program has developed considerable knowledge that has increased the security of energy control systems across the Nation. Since its inception, the program has formed valuable links between government, owners and operators, and national laboratories that help conduct R&D in the area of cybersecurity. Through these partnerships, the DOE/OE NSTB Program has identified ways to develop, integrate, and sustain security improvements.

[54] National Research Council, Committee on Science and Technology for Countering Terrorism, *Making the Nation Safer: The Role of Science and Technology in Countering Terrorism*, 2002, **www.nap.edu/catalog/10415.html?onpi_topnews090902**.

[55] RAND Corporation, unpublished workshop summary.

[56] **www.oe.energy.gov/DocumentsandMedia/roadmap.pdf**.

Table 7-1: Strategies for Securing Control Systems in the Energy Sector

Control Systems Roadmap Vision

In 10 years, control systems for critical applications will be designed, installed, operated, and maintained to survive an intentional cyber assault with no loss of critical function.

Challenges

- Limited ability to measure and assess cybersecurity posture
- No consistent cybersecurity metrics
- Hard to quantify and demonstrate threats
- Growing risks from increasingly interconnected systems

- Poorly designed connections of control systems and business networks
- Lack of clear design requirements
- Avoidance of performance degradation via security upgrades to legacy systems
- Increasingly sophisticated hacker tools

- Insufficient information sharing
- Poor industry-government coordination
- Weak business case for cybersecurity investments

Control Systems Roadmap Goals

Measure and Assess Security Posture	Develop and Integrate Protective Measures	Detect Intrusion and Implement Response Strategies	Sustain Security Improvements

Control Systems Roadmap Milestones

Near Term (0-2 Years)

• Baseline security methodologies, vulnerability assessments, and training available	• Consistent training materials on cyber and physical security for control systems widely available within the Energy Sector	• Incident reporting guidelines published and available throughout the Energy Sector	• Major info protection and sharing issues resolved between the U.S. government and industry • Industry-driven awareness campaign launched

Mid Term (2-5 Years)

• 50% of asset owners and operators performing vulnerability assessments of their control systems using consistent criteria • Common metrics available for benchmarking security posture • 90% of Energy Sector asset owners conducting internal compliance audits	• Communication between remote access devices and control centers secure • Field-proven best practices for control system security available • Secure connectivity between business systems and control systems within corporate network	• Cyber incident response in emergency operating plans at 30% of control systems • Commercial products in production that correlate all events across the enterprise network	• Secure forum for sharing cyber threat and response information • Compelling, evidence-based business case for investment in control systems security • Undergraduate curriculums, grants, and internships in control system security • Federal and state incentives to accelerate investment in technologies and practices

Long Term (5-10 Years)

• Real-time security state monitoring for new and legacy systems commercially available	• Non-destructive intrusion, isolation, and automated response exercises at 50% of control systems • Security test harness for evaluating next generation architectures and individual components	• Control system network models for contingency and remedial action in response to intrusions and anomalies • Self configuring control system network architectures in production	• Cybersecurity awareness, education, and outreach programs integrated into Energy Sector operations

End State (2015)

Energy asset owners are able to perform fully automated security state monitoring of their control system networks with real-time remediation	Next-generation control system components and architectures that offer built-in, end-to-end security will replace older legacy systems	Control system networks will automatically provide contingency and remedial actions in response to attempted intrusions	Energy asset owners and operators are working collaboratively with government and sector stakeholders to accelerate security advances

Figure 7-1: Key Accomplishments

Key Accomplishments to Meet Initial Roadmap Milestones

To date, NSTB and its industry partners have produced tangible results, including the following highlights:

· NSTB has assessed the majority of the current market offering of SCADA systems in the Electricity and the Oil and Gas subsectors.

· More than 1,900 end users have been trained by NSTB on best practices for control systems security.

· NSTB has conducted 21 on-site and test bed assessments, helping vendors to develop 11 hardened control systems designs.

· Development of the "ANTFARM" software: a no-cost tool that maps control system networks to help implement cybersecurity standards.

· The Bandolier project by Digital Bond, which has released audit files to help asset owners configure their control system applications according to security best practices.

· The Hallmark project by Schweitzer Engineering to commercialize a hardware device using the Secure SCADA Protocol developed by the Pacific Northwest National Laboratory to ensure message integrity.

· The AMI (Advanced Metering Infrastructure) Security Standards by the AMI-SEC Task Force provide utilities and vendors with a set of requirements to help secure implementation of AMI.

Expert panelists continued to advance this progress at the Roadmap Update Workshop in September 2009. More than 80 asset owners and operators, researchers, technology developers, security specialists, and equipment vendors in the public and private sectors renewed their commitment to the industry's vision and partnership efforts. The results of this workshop will enhance the 2006 Control Systems Roadmap and develop the 2010 Roadmap.

The Roadmap addressed the needs of the sector by establishing a vision and laying out a coherent plan for cybersecurity. The Roadmap envisions that "in 10 years, control systems for critical applications will be designed, installed, operated, and maintained to survive an intentional cyber assault with no loss of critical function." To achieve this vision, the Roadmap established a framework that is based on sound risk management principles and features the following four strategic goals:

1. *Measure and assess security posture.* Within 10 years, DOE, in coordination with sector partners, will help ensure that energy asset owners have the ability and commitment to perform fully automated monitoring of their control system networks' security with real-time remediation.

2. *Develop and integrate protective measures.* Within 10 years, next-generation control system components and architectures that offer built-in, end-to-end security will replace many older legacy systems.

3. *Detect intrusion and implement response strategies.* Within 10 years, DOE, in coordination with sector partners, will operate control system networks that automatically provide contingency and remedial actions in response to attempted intrusions into the control systems.

4. *Sustain security improvements.* Over the next 10 years, energy asset owners and operators are committed to working collaboratively with government and sector partners to accelerate security advances.

To help the industry track its progress in implementing the Roadmap, DOE created ieRoadmap, a Web-based tool that allows principal investigators to register and self-populate a database that links to the challenges identified in the Roadmap. The ieRoadmap provides a mechanism to encourage collaboration, identify active areas of work, expose gaps, and enable partners to leverage resources, as well as to inform owners and operators of emerging technologies.

After receiving positive feedback from Energy Sector partners on the Roadmap, the NERC CIPC voted unanimously to approve and support the implementation of the Roadmap. In addition, a 2007 report from the Government Accountability Office entitled, *Critical Infrastructure Protection: Multiple Efforts to Secure Control Systems Are Under Way, but Challenges Remain,*[57] commended the Roadmap efforts. The industry experts interviewed to develop the report stated the Roadmap was a "positive step for the industry" and the Roadmap process "succeeded in identifying industry needs and was a catalyst for bringing agencies and Government Coordinating Councils together."

7.2.2 Cybersecurity Programs

National Cyber Security for Energy Delivery Program. DOE supports the Roadmap primarily through its Control Systems Security Program, which conducts cybersecurity assessments of control systems and related technologies, develops advanced control system technologies, conducts modeling and simulation to better evaluate risk, and engages in industry partnership and outreach.

The program supports the NSTB Program, a suite of facilities that helps the sector owners and operators and equipment vendors test control systems to identify potential vulnerabilities. To date, the NSTB Program has conducted test-bed and on-site field vulnerability assessments of 15 control systems from vendors including ABB Group, Areva Group, General Electric Company (GE), Open Systems International, Inc. (OSI), Siemens USA, and Telvent. NSTB also conducted assessments of four control system component technologies. As a result, six next-generation "hardened" systems have been developed by the participating vendors, and at least 21 of one vendor's hardened systems have been deployed in the marketplace. Further, five software patches have been issued by participating vendors to address six critical security issues in response to vulnerabilities discovered by NSTB. One particular software patch issued by a vendor to secure its legacy systems has been downloaded by 82 utilities currently operating those systems. The Council on Competitiveness, in its 2007 report, *Transform Enterprise Resilience: The Resilient Economy; Integrating Competitiveness and Security*, stated that each control system assessed by NSTB "represents a class of more secure SCADA technology, creating a powerful multiplier effect on energy resilience nationwide."

System assessments have revealed common vulnerabilities and easy-to-implement, immediate security fixes that are applicable across the board. Outreach has helped disseminate this knowledge effectively. For example, more than 1,700 sector partners have participated in NSTB training workshops that educate system operators on effective security practices for control system security. In addition, NSTB partners with the NERC Control Systems Security Working Group to publish mitigations for the vulnerabilities identified in the annual report entitled, *Top 10 Vulnerabilities of Control Systems and Their Associated Mitigations*.

DOE has funded five industry projects to develop and integrate technologically advanced controls and cybersecurity devices into the Nation's electric grid and energy infrastructure:

1. *Hallmark Project*. To commercialize the Secure SCADA Communications Protocol (SSCP).
2. *Detection and Analysis of Threats to the Energy Sector (DATES)*. To develop an intrusion detection system (at the network, host, and device levels); an event correlation framework; and a sector-wide, distributed, privacy-preserving repository of security events to which participants can automatically contribute without attribution.

---

[57] GAO, *Critical Infrastructure Protection: Multiple Efforts to Secure Control Systems Are Under Way but Challenges Remain*, GAO-07-1036, September 2007, available at **www.gao.gov/cgi-bin/getrpt?GAO-07-1036**.

3. *Cyber Audit and Attack Detection Toolkit.* To extend the capability of existing vulnerability scanning tools to evaluate SCADA security configurations (supporting compliance with NERC CIP-005 and CIP-007) and to develop templates for a security event-monitoring system.

4. *Lemnos Interoperable Security Program.* To conduct testing, validation, and outreach to increase the availability of cost-effective, interoperable security solutions for Internet Protocol-based communications.

5. *Protecting Intelligent Distributed Power Grids against Cyber Attacks.* To develop a risk-based critical asset identification system and an integrated and distributed security system with optimization to establish the best topology for networking the security components.

One very promising technology to support the overall resilience of the grid is phasor technology, which is highlighted in figure 7-2.[58]

7.2.3 Cybersecurity Capability Gaps

The problem of securing the Nation's energy infrastructure is vast in scope and complexity. Some of the biggest challenges to achieving the vision outlined in the Roadmap include the following:

• *Keeping pace with the rapidly changing and growing threat environment.* New cyber vulnerabilities are discovered on a weekly basis. Sophisticated software tools, widely available on the Internet and sometimes traded for profit by cyber extortionists, allow hostile actors to develop and launch new cyber attacks faster than ever (even with limited control-system knowledge). The result is a vicious cycle in which there is a constant need for new countermeasures that require increasingly faster implementation.

• *Accelerating the commercialization of inherently secure and resilient control systems and Smart Grid technoligies.* As these systems become more integrated into enterprise- and corporate-wide systems, it is essential to transform the state of the art of control-system technology from an inherently insecure technology that requires layers of defense and costly management processes to a technology that provides built-in security and robustness. As Smart Grid technologies become an increasing part of the grid they must be secure from cyber attacks.

• *Increasing understanding of cyber risks.* While the understanding of the risk of cyber attacks on the energy infrastructure has been improved through Roadmap-related R&D, energy asset owners and operators still do not have the capabilities to fully understand the risks associated with the cyber threats of today and tomorrow. Without a better understanding of these risks, costs, and potential consequences, it will continue to be difficult to make a strong business case for cybersecurity investments.

---

[58] For more information about public and private sector projects, see the following:

• DOE NSTB Program, available at **http://www.oe.energy.gov/controlsecurity.htm**.
• Argonne National Laboratory, available at **http://www.dis.anl.gov/exp/ia/**.
• Idaho National Laboratory, available at **http://www.inl.gov/scada**.
• Oak Ridge National Laboratory, available at **http://www.ioc.ornl.gov/welcome.shtml**.
• PNNL, available at **http://www.pnl.gov/nationalsecurity/program/homeland/cyber_security/**.
• Sandia National Laboratories, available at **http://www.sandia.gov/scada**.
• DHS NCSD, available at **http://www.dhs.gov/xabout/structure/editorial_0839.shtm**.
• Process Control Systems Forum, available at **http://www.controlsystemsroadmap.net**.

On August 14, 2003, a cascading power failure left 50 million people in the northeastern United States and eastern Canada in the dark. It was the largest blackout in American history and prompted calls for better ways to monitor the nation's electric power system.

Through the collaborative leadership efforts of the DOE OE, NERC and electric utility companies, new sensors called phasor measurement units now provide simultaneous measurements of voltage, current, and frequency across a wide area of the grid. Phasors provide operators with a faster means to take the pulse of the nation's electric power grid. Phasors describe the differences in timing between the crests of the waveforms that characterize electrical power as it travels through the lines.

"If we had phasors in place then, we would have been able to see very clearly at least 30 minutes before that event that we were in trouble," said Stan Johnson, a manager at NERC, which is responsible for situational awareness and security of the electric power infrastructure. NERC sets mandatory reliability standards for how the North American electric grid is managed and enforces grid operator compliance with these standards. "We probably would have wound up shutting the lights off in the Cleveland, Ohio area, but at least [the blackout] would not have steamrolled all the way across the Northeast," Johnson said.

Power once came from relatively local sources. Now that new markets have opened, electricity from inexpensive or renewable sources that might be located in remote areas can be transmitted over long distances to densely populated regions with high power demands. As a result, bulk-power systems are operating much closer to their limits. Phase angles have long been used to assess the health of the grid, but these values were calculated from other measurements. With synchronized measurement devices placed directly on the lines and samples taken many times a second, those values can now be reported in real time, providing an instantaneous picture of the state of the grid.

DOE, NERC, and utility industry efforts continue to improve phasor technology and implement the use of phasor measurements throughout an increasing number of the thousands of miles of lines that supply the country with electric power.

Table 7-2 lists two key R&D capability requirements of the Energy Sector:

Table 7-2: R&D Gaps

Proposed Title of Requirement	Recovery Transformer
Goal/objective to which requirement responds	Energy SSP Physical and Cyber Security Goal 2: Use sound risk-management principles to implement physical and cyber measures that enhance preparedness, security, and resilience.
Theme	Advanced infrastructure architectures
Threat identification	The threat is failure of a high-voltage transformer through a physical or cyber attack; a new transformer can take 2 to 3 months to install and has a long manufacturing lead time (often more than 18 months), and there is limited/no domestic manufacturing capability.
Gaps of existing capabilities	There is a need for a new type of emergency spare (recovery/mobile) high-voltage transformer that can be deployed and energized quickly to rapidly recover from outages caused by natural disasters and deliberate attacks. A long term goal would be development of a solid state transformer.
Description of required operational capability	The recovery transformer must be able to be deployed and installed within days (e.g., 2 days to deliver and 2 days to energize), not months. Size/rating should be adaptable/modular to flexibly accommodate the needs of the utility industry.
Identification of existing related capabilities or technology	Previous research and analysis by DOE in high-temperature superconductivity, solid-state materials (power electronics), electrical steel, core design, and mobile transformers/substations could be leveraged to meet project objectives.
Identification of possible approaches/solutions	R&D, testing, and field demonstration of a single-phase high-voltage unit, at a minimum.

Proposed Title of Requirement	Cybersecurity for Control Systems
Goal/objective to which requirement responds	Energy SSP Physical and Cyber Security Goal 2: Use sound risk-management principles to implement physical and cyber measures that enhance preparedness, security, and resilience.
Theme	Protection and prevention systems
Threat identification	Energy sector control systems were originally designed for reliability, with little attention given to cybersecurity. Cyber threats are escalating, and the knowledge required to launch sophisticated attacks is decreasing.
Gaps of existing capabilities	The Roadmap to Secure Control Systems in the Energy Sector (January 2006) identifies the gaps in existing capabilities.

Proposed Title of Requirement	Cybersecurity for Control Systems
Description of required operational capability	The capabilities of the threat continue to evolve and adapt as new defenses are developed and deployed. Next-generation control systems are needed that can survive an intentional cyber assault with no loss of critical functions. Required operational capabilities include: · Fully automated security state monitoring with real-time remediation; · Components and architectures with built-in, end-to-end security; and · Automatic contingency and remedial actions in response to attempted intrusions.
Identification of existing related capabilities or technology	Previous R&D by the DOE NSTB Program in vulnerability assessments, advanced technologies, and risk analysis could be leveraged to meet the objectives.
Identification of possible approaches/solutions	R&D, testing, and field demonstration of control systems with cost-effective, hardened operating systems and secure, self-healing architectures that do not adversely affect overall system reliability, availability, and safety.

7.2.4 Physical Security R&D Requirements

The varied nature of assets in the Energy Sector suggests that the types of R&D needed to improve physical security (for all hazards) in the sector cover a far wider range than for cybersecurity. The physical assets themselves differ markedly between the Electricity and the Oil and Natural Gas subsectors. Further differences in protection opportunities are also evident among subsector components, such as substations versus transmission lines and refineries versus pipelines. While security technologies for physical assets are generally more mature than those for cyber systems, efforts to define the priority R&D needs to enhance the physical security of these diverse assets are likely to require several distinct, coordinated mapping efforts.

Using the sector partnership model, DOE and the Energy GCC will work with both Energy SCCs to identify the R&D opportunities for improving physical security of the energy infrastructure. The SCCs will play pivotal roles in defining and participating in the appropriate forums. Participation is vital due to the urgency of the potential threats to the Energy Sector, including multiple, coordinated physical and/or cyber attacks and electromagnetic pulse (EMP) events. These threats emphasize the need for tools and technologies that yield near-term responses to high-risk vulnerabilities. As resources are limited, support for activities (particularly near-term activities) has the potential to achieve a positive return on investment. The nature of threats and vulnerabilities is continually changing, a fact that also supports intermediate and long-range R&D.

7.3 Sector R&D Plan

Diverse public and private R&D initiatives are currently in progress to improve the Energy Sector's cybersecurity. DOE is working with other Federal agencies and industry groups to identify and map control system projects to R&D priorities identified in the Control Systems Roadmap. As future mapping efforts progress, new opportunities may be identified in addition to common activity areas where better coordination could optimize available resources. The resulting map will be used to align and guide ongoing government and industry activities, and will be updated periodically to track progress.

While formal mapping of R&D activities to address the physical security of Energy Sector assets awaits development, many important R&D activities are being conducted by industry and government. Consistent with the wide variation among assets, many of these activities are component-specific projects. As the Energy SCCs move forward to continue to develop R&D frameworks and mapping efforts, they will solicit active participation from a broad range of stakeholders (e.g., INGAA, Electric Power

Research Institute (EPRI), Gas Technology Institute (GTI), Pipeline Research Council International (PRCI), and National Electric Equipment Manufacturers Association (NEEMA)).

7.4 R&D Management Processes

Sector partners will pursue a focused, coordinated management approach that: (1) aligns current activities to R&D goals and milestones, (2) initiates specific projects to address critical gaps, and (3) provides a mechanism for collaboration, project management, and oversight. The aim of this approach is to accomplish clearly defined activities, projects, and initiatives that contain time-based deliverables that are tied to priority R&D requirements.

7.4.1 American Recovery and Reinvestment Act of 2009

The ARRA, which President Obama signed into law on February 17, 2009, is a response to a domestic economic crisis with significant implications for energy reliability, sustainability, and resilience. It includes significant measures to modernize the Nation's energy and communication infrastructure and enhance energy independence.

The ARRA includes $4.5 billion for DOE/OE. As outlined in the legislation, the funds are an investment in a nationwide plan to modernize the electric grid, enhance security of U.S. energy infrastructure, and ensure reliable electricity delivery to meet growing demand. This represents a significant increase in DOE's investment in grid modernization and reflects a recognition that a more efficient and integrated grid is integral to achieving President Obama's goals to significantly increase use of renewable energy resources and improve the Nation's economic future.

The funds primarily support implementation of the Smart Grid programs authorized by the Energy Independence and Security Act of 2007. These include the Smart Grid technology research, development and demonstration projects authorized in section 1304, and the federal matching fund for Smart Grid technologies in section 1306. A significant share of the funds will be used to support these programs through a competitive grant process. As a result of DOE/OE's ARRA efforts, DOE anticipates impacting more than 36,000 jobs.

8. Managing and Coordinating SSA Responsibilities

As the SSA for energy, DOE bears primary responsibility for enhancing the resilience of the Nation's critical energy infrastructure. This responsibility requires DOE to take on several major roles. First, in cooperation with DHS and other government agencies, DOE provides situational awareness to energy stakeholders. In the face of a possible threat to the energy infrastructure, energy emergency, disruption, or other significant event affecting the Nation's energy supply, DOE strives to supply timely information. Second, DOE works with DHS and other Energy GCC partners to help clarify and coordinate the roles of sector partners and facilitate cooperation with energy stakeholders. This is intended to help reduce the burden on industry, and eliminate unnecessary duplication of effort as much as possible. These efforts are also intended to increase information sharing between government partners and between government and energy asset owners and operators. Third, DOE, with support from DHS and other Energy GCC members, works to improve coordination of resilience activities among sector partners and between energy and other CIKR sectors.

Within DOE, these functions are the responsibility of the ISER of the OE. Simply put, the mission of OE/ISER is to support the efforts that ensure the reliability, survivability, and resilience of the Nation's critical energy infrastructure.

8.1 Program Management Approach

OE will manage and coordinate DOE's responsibilities as the SSA for energy, including those responsibilities and activities associated with the NIPP and the Energy SSP. This structure will be assessed annually during the Energy Sector annual reporting process, and during any planned updates of the Energy SSP.

In keeping with the public-private partnership model, DOE, DHS, and other Federal, State, and local government partners continue to work closely with their industry partners to manage the SSP process and its implementation. DOE does not view this as a government program, but rather as a joint government-industry activity.

8.2 Processes and Responsibilities

8.2.1 SSP Maintenance and Update

DOE works closely with its partners in both the electricity and the oil and natural gas industries to update the SSP as required. The Energy Sector Annual Report to DHS describes ongoing activities and developments. This 2010 Energy SSP is the first update to the Energy SSP, and it supports the 2009 *National Infrastructure Protection Plan — Partnering to Enhance Protection and Resiliency*. During development of the current Energy SSP sector partners determined that the underlying vision and goals should remain the same. Some areas, including cyber and pandemic concerns, have been given additional focus. DOE and its partners, through the SSP review process, have made updates and changes in coordination with DHS and other government energy partners. Throughout this process, the DOE program manager has maintained version control and managed the review process. DOE, as the SSA for energy, continues to have the lead for maintaining and updating the plan, in close collaboration with partners throughout the sector.

In executing this process, DOE continues to work through the SCCs for electricity and oil and natural gas, which include private industry partners, and the Energy GCC, which includes representatives from other Federal agencies, and State, local, territorial, and tribal governments.

8.2.2 Annual Reporting

In accordance with DHS requirements, DOE has and will continue to submit an Energy Sector CIKR Protection Annual Report. The first of these reports was submitted in July 2006. DOE program managers oversee production of this annual report in close coordination with sector partners. Coordination with appropriate sector partners will continue to be managed through the Oil and Natural Gas and Electricity SCCs, CIPAC working groups, and the GCC.

8.2.3 Resources and Budgets

The entire DOE/OE budget for operations and analysis supports the objectives of the SSP. The 2009 ARRA "Smart Grid" grants provide additional budgetary support for the goals in the Energy SSP, as they are designed to enhance the efficiency and resilience of the Nation's power grid. DOE will continue to work with its sector partners as appropriate to help them develop investment priorities and requirements for CIKR protection, restoration, and recovery. DOE and DHS R&D also support industry efforts to improve energy infrastructure reliability and resilience in the face of physical and cyber threats (including those from natural hazards), as well as threats from HILF events such as EMP, earthquakes, or pandemics.

8.2.4 Training and Education

Successful implementation of the NIPP risk management framework relies on building and maintaining individual and organizational CIKR protection and recovery expertise. Training and education in a variety of areas are necessary to achieve and sustain this level of expertise.

DOE works with DHS and industry SCC members and trade associations to support development of effective training programs, and to encourage widespread participation and buy-in through various industry participants. Many industry partners have sophisticated, well-developed training programs already in place, both at the company level and through industry groups. Some training, such as that for gas controllers, is mandated by regulation. NERC establishes training and certification requirements for the Electricity subsector. DOE has supported training for State and local government through programs offered by NASEO, NARUC, NSCL, and NGA. These opportunities have included regional training for public utility commissions by NARUC, Web-based training for EEACs offered by NASEO, and workshops and presentations conducted at meetings and conferences across the United States. In addition, regional energy emergency exercises are currently being offered.

The NIPP lists some of the areas of expertise where training is recommended,[59] examples of available training, and other general information on CIKR protection-related training and education. DOE will continue to work with DHS and other sector partners to identify training needs.[60]

---

[59] See section 6.2 of the NIPP.

[60] For further discussions, see section 6.2 of the NIPP, pp. 80-83.

8.3 Information Sharing and Protection

Chapter 5 of this SSP describes various mechanisms currently in place for energy partners to share and protect information. Considerable progress has been made in these efforts. As the SSA for energy, DOE is responsible for collaboration with private sector partners, as well as for encouraging development of appropriate information-sharing and analysis processes and mechanisms to support these processes. DOE is undertaking these efforts with a particular focus on protection of sensitive information regarding physical and cyber threats, vulnerabilities, incidents, recommended protective measures, and security-related effective practices. The primary objective of the NIPP networked approach to information sharing is to maximize the ability of government and private sector partners at all levels to assess risks and execute risk mitigation programs and activities.[61]

Specific information-sharing and protection plans already exist, including the ESISAC, HSIN, and ISERnet. Other mechanisms will be developed as DOE continues to work with its partners. All efforts will be made to facilitate communication between DOE, the SCCs, governmental and private sector partners, and international partners, as appropriate. This includes the prompt and effective transmission of actionable intelligence and threat information to sector partners.

8.4 Implementing the Partnership Model

8.4.1 Partnership Coordination and Efficiency

DOE, DHS, and the Energy Sector GCC play very important roles under the Energy SSP in terms of coordination and efficiency of partnership activities. The SCCs represent the private sector's participation in securing the Nation's energy infrastructure. From a private sector perspective, it is important that all Federal voluntary efforts involving sector owners and operators be carefully coordinated to create an efficient partnership model that will consolidate and prioritize the multiple voluntary Federal initiatives under the sector, and that will also recognize the breadth and scope of all Federal regulatory initiatives (e.g., CFATS) that similarly impact the sector.

All voluntary activities under the Energy SSP need to be supportive of the sector vision and goals in section 1.1, as well as the value proposition in section 1.4. Partnership activities should also complement, not supplant, the breadth of existing owner/operator, trade association, and sector activities and programs already in place.

Cross-sector initiatives by DHS (e.g., Protective Security Advisor reviews of private sector systems and assets) or other agency partners should provide feedback to DOE and its partners. Cross-sector and topic-specific data collections by DHS should similarly be coordinated and prioritized with DOE and its sector partners. Additional efforts should be taken to consolidate the multiple, independent data collection activities that occur under the NIPP framework.

---

[61] See section 4.2 of the NIPP.

Appendix 1: Glossary of Key Terms

Many of the definitions in this glossary come directly from the NIPP, and as such, are derived from language enacted in Federal laws and/or included in national plans, including the Homeland Security Act of 2002, the USA PATRIOT Act of 2001, the National Incident Management System, and the National Response Framework. Additional definitions come from the DHS and DOE lexicon.

All-Hazards. A grouping classification encompassing all conditions, environmental or manmade, that have the potential to cause injury, illness, or death; damage to or loss of equipment, infrastructure services, or property; or alternatively causing functional degradation to social, economic, or environmental aspects.

Asset. A person, structure, facility, information, material, or process that has value. In the context of the NIPP, people are not considered assets.

Business Continuity. The ability of an organization to continue to function before, during, and after a disaster.

Chemical Facility Anti-Terrorism Standards (CFATS). Section 550 of the DHS Appropriations Act of 2007 grants the Department of Homeland Security the authority to regulate chemical facilities that "present high levels of security risk." The CFATS establish a risk-informed approach to screening and securing chemical facilities determined by DHS to be "high risk."

CIKR Partner. Those Federal, State, local, tribal, or territorial governmental entities; public and private sector owners and operators and representative organizations; regional organizations and coalitions; academic and professional entities; and certain not-for-profit and private volunteer organizations that share in the responsibility for protecting the Nation's CIKR.

Consequence. The effect of an event, incident, or occurrence. For the purposes of the NIPP, consequences are divided into four main categories: public health and safety, economic, psychological, and governance impacts.

Control Center. A sophisticated monitoring and control system responsible for balancing power generation and demand; monitoring flows over transmission lines to avoid overloading; planning and configuring the system to operate reliably; maintaining system stability; preparing for emergencies; and placing equipment in and out of service for maintenance and emergencies.

Control Systems. Computer-based systems used within many infrastructures and industries to monitor and control sensitive processes and physical functions. These systems typically collect measurement and operational data from the field, process and display the information, and relay control commands to local or remote equipment or human-machine interfaces (operators). Examples of types of control systems include SCADA systems, Process Control Systems, and Distributed Control Systems.

Critical Infrastructure. Systems and assets, whether physical or virtual, so vital that the incapacity or destruction of such may have a debilitating impact on the security, economy, public health or safety, environment, or any combination of these matters, across any Federal, State, regional, territorial, or local jurisdiction.

Critical Infrastructure Information (CII). Information that is not customarily in the public domain and is related to the security of critical infrastructure or protected systems. CII consists of records and information concerning any of the following:

- Actual, potential, or threatened interference with, attack on, compromise of, or incapacitation of critical infrastructure or protected systems by either physical or computer-based attack or other similar conduct (including the misuse of or unauthorized access to all types of communications and data transmission systems) that violates Federal, State, or local law; harms the interstate commerce of the United States; or threatens public health or safety.

- The ability of any critical infrastructure or protected system to resist such interference, compromise, or incapacitation, including any planned or past assessment, projection, or estimate of the vulnerability of critical infrastructure or a protected system, including security testing, risk evaluation thereto, risk management planning, or risk audit.

- Any planned or past operational problem or solution regarding critical infrastructure or protected systems, including repair, recovery, insurance, or continuity, to the extent that it is related to such interference, compromise, or incapacitation.

Cybersecurity. The prevention of damage to, unauthorized use of, or exploitation of, and, if needed, the restoration of electronic information and communications systems and the information contained therein to ensure confidentiality, integrity, and availability. Includes protection and restoration, when needed, of information networks and wireline, wireless, satellite, public safety answering points, and 911 communications systems and control systems.

Cyber System. Any combination of facilities, equipment, personnel, procedures, and communications integrated to provide cyber services. Examples include business systems, control systems, and access control systems.

Dependency. The one-directional reliance of an asset, system, network, or collection thereof, within or across sectors, on input, interaction, or other requirement from other sources in order to function properly.

Electromagnetic Pulse (EMP). A burst of electromagnetic radiation by deliberate means, such as nuclear attack, or through natural means, such as a large-scale geomagnetic storm. Magnetic and electric fields resulting from EMP have the potential to disrupt electrical and electronic systems by causing destructive current and voltage surges.

Energy Asset and System Parameters. Six general asset or system characteristics that are important parameters for evaluating the vulnerabilities of energy infrastructure and developing risk management programs. They include: physical and location attributes, cyber attributes, volumetric or throughput attributes, temporal/load profile attributes, human attributes, and the importance of an asset or system to the energy network.

Function. A service, process, capability, or operation performed by an asset, system, network, or organization.

Government Coordinating Council. The government counterpart to the SCC for each sector established to enable interagency coordination. The GCC comprises representatives across various levels of government (Federal, State, local, tribal, and territorial) as appropriate to the security and operational landscape of each individual sector.

Hazard. A natural or manmade source or cause of harm or difficulty.

High-Impact, Low-Frequency (HILF). HILF events are occurrences that are relatively unusual, but have the potential to cause catastrophic disruption. Examples include pandemic disease, terrorist attack, and electromagnetic pulse

Homeland Security Information Network (HSIN). The Homeland Security Information Network is a comprehensive, nationally secure and trusted web-based platform able to facilitate Sensitive But Unclassified (SBU) information sharing and collaboration between Federal, State, local, tribal, territorial, private sector, and international partners.

Homeland Security Presidential Directive 7 (HSPD-7). Homeland Security Presidential Directive 7 establishes a national policy for Federal departments and agencies to identify and prioritize critical infrastructure and to protect them from terrorist attacks. The directive defines relevant terms and delivers 31 policy statements. These policy statements define what the directive covers and the roles various Federal, State, and local agencies will play in carrying it out.

Incident. An occurrence, caused by either human action or natural phenomena, that may cause harm and may require action. Incidents can include major disasters, emergencies, terrorist attacks, terrorist threats, wild and urban fires, floods, hazardous materials spills, nuclear accidents, aircraft accidents, earthquakes, hurricanes, tornadoes, tropical storms, war-related disasters, public health and medical emergencies, and other occurrences requiring an emergency response.

Infrastructure. The framework of interdependent networks and systems comprising identifiable industries, institutions, (including people and procedures), and distribution capabilities that provide a reliable flow of products and services essential to the defense and economic security of the United States, the smooth functioning of government at all levels, and society as a whole. Consistent with the definition in the Homeland Security Act, infrastructure includes physical, cyber, and/or human elements.

Interdependency. Mutually reliant relationship between entities (objects, individuals, or groups). The degree of interdependency does not need to be equal in both directions.

Key Resources. As defined in the Homeland Security Act, key resources are publicly or privately controlled resources essential to the minimal operations of the economy and government.

Mitigation. Ongoing and sustained action to reduce the probability of or lessen the impact of an adverse incident.

National Infrastructure Advisory Council (NIAC). An organization that provides the President, through the Secretary of Homeland Security, with advice on the security of the critical infrastructure sectors and their information systems. The council is composed of a maximum of 30 members, appointed by the President from private industry, academia, and State and local government.

Network. A group of components that share information or interact with each other in order to perform a function.

Owners/Operators. Those entities responsible for day-to-day operation and investment in a particular asset or system.

Pandemic Influenza. Defined by the World Health Organization (WHO) as a global outbreak of influenza, characterized by an emergent strain of the virus, little to no immunity among the general population, rapid and sustained person-to-person transmission, and lack of a vaccine. On June 11, 2009, WHO determined that 2009 H1N1 influenza (also known as "swine flu") had reached pandemic status.

Physical Security. The use of barriers and surveillance to protect resources, personnel, and facilities against crime, damage, or unauthorized access.

Preparedness. The activities necessary to build, sustain, and improve readiness capabilities to prevent, protect against, respond to, and recover from natural or manmade incidents. Preparedness is a continuous process involving efforts at all levels of government and between government and the private sector and nongovernmental organizations to identify threats, determine vulnerabilities, and identify required resources to prevent, respond to, and recover from major incidents.

Prevention. Actions taken and measures put in place for the continual assessment and readiness of necessary actions to reduce the risk of threats and vulnerabilities, to intervene and stop an occurrence, or to mitigate effects.

Prioritization. In the context of the NIPP, prioritization is the process of using risk assessment results to identify where risk reduction or mitigation efforts are most needed and to subsequently determine which protective actions should be instituted in order to have the greatest effect.

Protected Critical Infrastructure Information (PCII). PCII refers to all critical infrastructure information, including categorical inclusion PCII, that has undergone the validation process and that the PCII Program Office has determined qualifies for protection under the CII Act. All information submitted to the PCII Program Office or Designee with an express statement is presumed to be PCII until the PCII Program Office determines otherwise.

Protection. Actions or measures taken to cover or shield from exposure, injury, or destruction. In the context of the NIPP, protection includes actions to deter the threat, mitigate the vulnerabilities, or minimize the consequences associated with a terrorist attack or other incident. Protection can include a wide range of activities, such as hardening facilities, building resilience and redundancy, incorporating hazard resistance into initial facility design, initiating active or passive countermeasures, installing security systems, promoting workforce surety, training and exercises, and implementing cybersecurity measures, among various others.

Protective Security Advisor (PSA). A field-based liaison between DHS and the State and local CIKR protection community. Using site visits and cross-sector analysis, PSAs identify, assess, monitor, and minimize risks to CIKR assets at the local or district level.

Recovery. The development, coordination, and execution of service- and site-restoration plans for affected communities and the reconstitution of government operations and services through individual, private sector, nongovernmental, and public assistance programs that identify needs and define resources; provide housing and promote restoration; address long-term care and treatment of affected persons; implement additional measures for community restoration; incorporate mitigation measures and techniques, as feasible; evaluate the incident to identify lessons learned; and develop initiatives to mitigate the effects of future incidents.

Redundancy. An energy reliability strategy based on the notion that multiple systems provide needed backup if one system fails or cannot meet demand.

Resilience/Resiliency. The ability to resist, absorb, recover from, or successfully adapt to adversity or a change in conditions. In the context of energy security, resilience is measured in terms of robustness, resourcefulness, and rapid recovery.

Response. Activities that address the short-term, direct effects of an incident, including immediate actions to save lives, protect property, and meet basic human needs. Response also includes the execution of emergency operations plans and incident mitigation activities designed to limit the loss of life, personal injury, property damage, and other unfavorable outcomes. As indicated by the situation, response activities include applying intelligence and other information to lessen the effects or consequences of an incident; increasing security operations; continuing investigations into the nature and source of the threat; ongoing surveillance and testing processes; immunizations, isolation, or quarantine; and specific law enforcement operations aimed at preempting, interdicting, or disrupting illegal activity, and apprehending actual perpetrators and bringing them to justice.

Risk. The potential for an unwanted outcome resulting from an incident, event, or occurrence, as determined by its likelihood and the associated consequences.

Risk Management Framework. A planning methodology that outlines the process for setting goals and objectives; identifying assets, systems, and networks; assessing risks; prioritizing and implementing protection programs and resilience strategies; measuring performance; and taking corrective action. Public and private entities often include risk management frameworks in their business continuity plans.

Roadmap to Secure Control Systems in the Energy Sector (Roadmap). The DOE and DHS sponsored document that outlines a coherent plan for improving cybersecurity in the Energy Sector, identifying concrete steps to secure control systems used in the Electricity, Oil, and Natural Gas subsectors over a ten-year period. First published in 2006, the Roadmap will be updated in 2010.

Sector. A logical collection of assets, systems, or networks that provide a common function to the economy, government, or society. The NIPP addresses 18 CIKR sectors, identified by the criteria set forth in HSPD-7.

Sector Coordinating Council (SCC). The private sector counterpart to the GCC, these councils are self-organized, self-run, and self-governed organizations that are representative of a spectrum of key stakeholders within a sector. SCCs serve as the government's principal point of entry into each sector for developing and coordinating a wide range of CIKR protection activities and issues.

Sector Partnership Model. The framework used to promote and facilitate sector and cross-sector planning, coordination, collaboration, and information sharing for CIKR protection involving all levels of government and private sector entities.

Sector-Specific Agency (SSA). Federal departments and agencies identified in HSPD-7 as responsible for CIKR protection activities in specified CIKR sectors.

Sector-Specific Plans (SSP). Augmenting plans that complement and extend the NIPP and detail the application of the NIPP framework specific to each CIKR sector. SSPs are developed by the SSAs in close collaboration with other sector partners.

Situational Awareness. An understanding of the current environment and the ability to accurately anticipate future problems in order to respond effectively.

Smart Grid. The electric delivery network, from electrical generation to end-use customer, integrated with the latest advances in digital and information technology to improve electric-system reliability, security, and efficiency.

Supply Chain. In the Energy Sector, a system of interdependent processes and assets that includes the extraction of raw material, the refinement and transportation of fuel, the generation, transmission, and distribution of electricity, and the delivery of energy, in its various forms, to the end-use consumer.

System. Any combination of facilities, equipment, personnel, procedures, and communications integrated for a specific purpose.

Terrorism. Premeditated threat or act of violence against non-combatant persons, property, and environmental or economic targets to induce fear, intimidate, coerce, or affect a government, the civilian population, or any segment thereof, in furtherance of political, social, ideological, or religious objectives.

Threat. A natural or manmade occurrence, individual, entity, or action that has or indicates the potential to harm life, information, operations, the environment, and/or property.

Value Proposition. A statement that outlines the national and homeland security interest in protecting the Nation's CIKR and articulates the benefits gained by all CIKR partners through the risk management framework and public-private partnership described in the NIPP.

Vulnerability. A physical feature or operational attribute that renders an entity open to exploitation or susceptible to a given hazard.

Appendix 2: List of Acronyms and Abbreviations

AGA	American Gas Association
AMSC	Area Maritime Security Committees
AOPL	Association of Oil Pipe Lines
APGA	American Public Gas Association
API	American Petroleum Institute
APPA	American Public Power Association
ARRA	American Reinvestment and Recovery Act of 2009
BOR	Bureau of Reclamation
BPA	Bonneville Power Administration
BZPP	Buffer Zone Protection Program
CEC	California Energy Commission
CII Act	Critical Infrastructure Information Act
CIKR	Critical Infrastructure and Key Resources
CIP	Critical Infrastructure Protection
CIPAC	Critical Infrastructure Partnership Advisory Council
CIPC	Critical Infrastructure Protection Committee
DCS	Digital Control Systems
DHS	Department of Homeland Security
DOC	Department of Commerce
DoD	Department of Defense
DOE	Department of Energy
DOI	Department of the Interior
DOS	Department of State
DOT	Department of Transportation
DPA	Defense Production Act

EEAC	Energy Emergency Assurance Coordinators
EEI	Edison Electric Institute
EIA	Energy Information Administration
EIAC	Energy Industry Assurance Coordinators
EMS	Energy Management Systems
EPA	Environmental Protection Agency
EPCA	Energy Policy and Conservation Act
EPRI	Electric Power Research Institute
ERO	Energy Reliability Organization
ESCC	Electricity Sector Coordinating Council
ESF	Emergency Support Function
ESISAC	Electricity Sector Information Sharing and Analysis Center
FACA	Federal Advisory Committee Act
FBI	Federal Bureau of Investigation
FEMA	Federal Emergency Management Agency
FERC	Federal Energy Regulatory Commission
FISMA	Federal Information Security Management Act
FOIA	Freedom of Information Act
FPA	Federal Power Act
FUA	Power Plant and Industrial Fuel Use Act
GCC	Government Coordinating Council
GTI	Gas Technology Institute
HITRAC	Homeland Infrastructure Threat and Risk Analysis Center
HSAS	Homeland Security Advisory System
HSIN	Homeland Security Information Network
HSPD	Homeland Security Presidential Directive
IEP	International Energy Program
INGAA	Interstate Natural Gas Association of America
IP	Office of Infrastructure Protection
ISAC	Information Sharing and Analysis Center
ISER	Infrastructure Security and Energy Restoration
ISO	Independent System Operator
LNG	Liquefied Natural Gas
MISO	Midwest Independent System Operator
MMS	Minerals Management Service

MOU	Memorandum of Understanding
MTSA	Maritime Transportation Security Act
NAESB	North American Energy Standards Board
NAEWG	North American Energy Working Group
NARUC	National Association of Regulatory Utility Commissioners
NASEO	National Association of State Energy Officials
NCS	National Communications System
NCSD	National Cyber Security Division
NCSL	National Conference of State Legislatures
NEMA	National Emergency Management Association
NEPA	National Environmental Policy Act
NERC	North American Electric Reliability Corporation
NGA	National Governors Association
NIPP	National Infrastructure Protection Plan
NPC	National Petroleum Council
NPGA	National Propane Gas Association
NPRA	National Petrochemical and Refining Association
NRC	Nuclear Regulatory Commission
NRCan	Natural Resources Canada
NRECA	National Rural Electric Cooperative Association
NRF	National Response Framework
NSEP	National Security Emergency Preparedness
NSF	National Science Foundation
NTSB	National Transportation Safety Board
NYISO	New York Independent System Operator
NYMEX	New York Mercantile Exchange
OE	Office of Electricity Delivery and Energy Reliability
ONG SCC	Oil and Natural Gas Sector Coordinating Council
PCII	Protected Critical Infrastructure Information Program
PHMSA	Pipeline and Hazardous Material Safety Administration
PMA	Power Marketing Administrations
PNWER	Pacific Northwest Economic Region
PRCI	Pipeline Research Council International
PSEPC	Public Safety and Emergency Preparedness Canada
PTI	Public Technology Institute

PURPA	Public Utilities Regulatory Policy Act
RAM-T[SM]	Risk Assessment Methodology for Transmission
R&D	Research & Development
RTO	Regional Transmission Organization
S&T	Science & Technology Directorate
SCADA	Supervisory Control and Data Acquisition
SCC	Sector Coordinating Council
SIP	State Implementation Plan
SPR	Strategic Petroleum Reserve
SSA	Sector-Specific Agency
SSP	Sector-Specific Plan
TISP	The Infrastructure Security Partnership
TSA	Transportation Security Administration
TSI	Threats and Suspicious Incidents
TSSP	Transportation Sector-Specific Plan
TSWG	Technical Support Working Group
TVA	Tennessee Valley Authority
TWIC	Transportation Worker Identification Cards
USACE	United States Army Corps of Engineers
USCG	United States Coast Guard
USDA	United States Department of Agriculture
VMWG	Visualization and Modeling Working Group
WAPA	Washington Area Power Association

Appendix 3: Sources and References

American Gas Association (AGA), **www.aga.org**

American Petroleum Institute (API), **www.api.org**

American Public Gas Association (APGA), **www.apga.org**

American Public Power Association (APPA), **www.appanet.org**

American Recovery and Reinvestment Act of 2009 (ARRA),
http://frwebgate.access.gpo.gov/cgi-bin/getdoc.cgi?dbname=111_cong_bills&docid=f:h1enr.pdf

Association of Oil Pipe Lines (AOPL), **www.aopl.org**

Bonneville Power Administration (BPA), **www.bpa.gov**

California Energy Commission (CEC), **www.energy.ca.gov**

Canadian Electricity Association (CEA), **www.canelect.ca**

Centers for Disease Control and Prevention (CDC), **http://www.cdc.gov/**

Chemical Facility Anti-Terrorism Standards (CFATS), **http://www.dhs.gov/files/laws/gc_1166796969417.shtm**

Critical Infrastructure Information Act of 2002 (CII Act), **www.dhs.gov/xlibrary/assets/CII_Act.pdf**

Critical Infrastructure Partnership Advisory Council (CIPAC), **http://www.dhs.gov/files/committees/editorial_0843.shtm**

Cyberspace Policy Review: Assuring a Trusted and Resilient Information and Communications Infrastructure, 2009,
http://www.whitehouse.gov/assets/documents/Cyberspace_Policy_Review_final.pdf

Defense Production Act (DPA) Reauthorization of 2009,
http://frwebgate.access.gpo.gov/cgi-bin/getdoc.cgi?dbname=111_cong_public_laws&docid=f:publ067.111

Edison Electric Institute (EEI), **www.eei.org**

Energy Independence and Security Act of 2007,
http://frwebgate.access.gpo.gov/cgi-bin/getdoc.cgi?dbname=110_cong_bills&docid=f:h6enr.txt.pdf

Electric Power Research Institute (EPRI), **www.epri.com**

Electricity Sector Information Sharing and Analysis Center (ESISAC), **www.esisac.com**

Energy Policy Act of 2005 (EPAct 2005),
http://frwebgate.access.gpo.gov/cgi-bin/getdoc.cgi?dbname=109_cong_bills&docid=f:h6enr.txt.pdf

Energy Reliability Organization (ERO), **www.ferc.gov/news/news-releases/2006/2006-3/07-20-06-E-5.pdf**

Federal Emergency Management Agency (FEMA), **www.fema.gov**

Federal Energy Regulatory Commission (FERC), **www.ferc.gov**

Final Report on the August 14th Blackout in the United States and Canada (Blackout Report), **https://reports.energy.gov**

Gas Technology Institute (GTI), **www.gastechnology.org**

Homeland Security Advisory System (HSAS), **www.dhs.gov/xinfoshare/programs/Copy_of_press_release_0046.shtm**

Homeland Security Information Network (HSIN), **www.dhs.gov/xinfoshare/programs/gc_1156888108137.shtm**

Homeland Security Presidential Directive 7 (HSPD-7), **www.dhs.gov/xabout/laws/gc_1214597989952.shtm**

Infrastructure Security and Energy Restoration (ISER), **www.oe.energy.gov/our_organization/iser.htm**

Interstate Natural Gas Association of America (INGAA), **www.ingaa.org**

Minerals Management Service (MMS), **www.mms.gov**

National Association of Regulatory Utility Commissioners (NARUC), **www.naruc.org**

National Association of State Energy Officials (NASEO), **www.naseo.org**

National Conference of State Legislatures (NCSL), **www.ncsl.org**

National Governors Association (NGA), **www.nga.org**

National Infrastructure Advisory Council (NIAC), **http://www.dhs.gov/files/committees/editorial_0353.shtm**

National Infrastructure Protection Plan (NIPP), **http://www.dhs.gov/files/programs/editorial_0827.shtm**

National Petrochemical and Refiners Association (NPRA), **www.npradc.org**

National Propane Gas Association (NPGA), **www.npga.org**

National Rural Electric Cooperative Association (NRECA), **www.nreca.org**

National SCADA Test Bed, **http://www.oe.energy.gov/nstb.htm**

National Science Foundation (NSF), **www.nsf.gov**

Natural Resources Canada (NRCan), **www.nrcan.gc.ca**

NERC Critical Infrastructure Protection Committee (CIPC), **www.nerc.com/page.php?cid=1%7C9%7C117%7C139**

NERC Reliability Standards, **http://www.nerc.com/page.php?cid=2|20**

North American Electric Reliability Corporation (NERC), **www.nerc.com**

North American Energy Standards Board (NAESB), **www.naesb.org**

North American Energy Working Group (NAEWG), **www.eia.doe.gov/emeu/northamerica/engnaewg.htm#_VPID_1**

Nuclear Regulatory Commission (NRC), **www.nrc.gov**

Office of Electricity Delivery and Energy Reliability (OE), **www.oe.energy.gov**

Office of Science and Technology Policy (OSTP), **www.ostp.gov**

Pacific Northwest Economic Region (PNWER), **www.pnwer.org**

Pipeline and Hazardous Materials Safety Administration (PHMSA), **www.phmsa.dot.gov**

Power Marketing Administration (PMA), **www.energy.gov/organization/powermarketingadmin.htm**

Protected Critical Infrastructure Information (PCII) Program, **www.dhs.gov/xinfoshare/programs/editorial_0404.shtm**

Public Safety Canada, **http://www.publicsafety.gc.ca/index-eng.aspx**

Public Technology Institute (PTI), **www.pti.org**

Regional Transmission Organizations (RTO)/Independent System Operators (ISO), **www.ferc.gov/industries/electric/indus-act/rto.asp**

Roadmap to Secure Control Systems in the Energy Sector (Roadmap), **http://www.oe.energy.gov/csroadmap.htm**

Robert T. Stafford Disaster Relief and Emergency Assistance Act, as amended, **http://www.fema.gov/pdf/about/stafford_act.pdf**

Smart Grid, **http://www.oe.energy.gov/smartgrid.htm**

Strategic Petroleum Reserve (SPR), **www.spr.doe.gov**

Technical Support Working Group (TSWG), **www.tswg.gov**

Tennessee Valley Authority (TVA), **www.tva.gov**

The Electric Distribution Program (GridWise Program), **www.electricdistribution.ctc.com/index.htm**

The Infrastructure Security Partnership (TISP), **www.tisp.org/tisp.cfm**

Transportation Security Administration (TSA), **www.tsa.gov**

United States Army Corps of Engineers (USACE), **www.usace.army.mil**

United States Coast Guard (USCG), **www.uscg.mil**

United States Department of Agriculture (USDA), **www.usda.gov**

United States Department of Commerce (DOC), **www.commerce.gov**

United States Department of Defense (DoD), **www.defenselink.mil**

United States Department of Energy (DOE), **www.doe.gov**

United States Department of Energy, Energy Information Administration (EIA), **www.eia.doe.gov**

United States Department of Health and Human Services (HHS), **http://www.hhs.gov/**

United States Department of Homeland Security (DHS), **http://www.dhs.gov/index.shtm**

United States Department of the Interior (DOI), **www.doi.gov**

United States Department of the Interior, Bureau of Reclamation (BOR), **www.usbr.gov**

United States Department of State (DOS), **www.state.gov**

United States Department of Transportation (DOT), **www.dot.gov**

United States Environmental Protection Agency (EPA), **www.epa.gov**

Western Area Power Administration (WAPA), **www.wapa.gov**

Appendix 4: Authorities

American Recovery and Reinvestment Act of 2009, Public Law 111-5

The ARRA granted supplemental appropriations for Fiscal Year 2009 to DOE for, among other things, programs for energy efficiency and renewable energy, electricity delivery and energy reliability, and fossil energy research and development. Section 405 specifically provides financial support for Smart Grid demonstration projects in urban, suburban, tribal, and rural areas, as well as to electric utilities that invest in advanced grid technology. This section also requires the Secretary of Energy to establish and maintain a Smart Grid information clearinghouse which will make data from Smart Grid demonstration projects and other sources available to the public. The ARRA provides a number of additional financial incentives for renewable energy, energy efficiency, and biomass projects on the State, local, and individual level.

Homeland Security Presidential Directive 5 (HSPD-5)

This directive enhances the ability of the United States to manage domestic incidents by establishing a single, comprehensive National Incident Management System. It requires all Federal departments and agencies to cooperate with the Secretary of Homeland Security by providing their full and prompt cooperation, resources, and support, as appropriate and consistent with their own responsibilities for protecting the Nation's security. The directive provides for Federal assistance to State and local authorities when their resources are overwhelmed, or when Federal interests are involved.

Homeland Security Presidential Directive 7 (HSPD-7)

This directive establishes a national policy for Federal departments and agencies to identify and prioritize U.S. CIKR and protect them from terrorist attacks. Federal departments and agencies are required to: (1) identify, prioritize, and coordinate CIKR protection to prevent, deter, and mitigate the effects of deliberate efforts to destroy, incapacitate, or exploit them; and (2) work with State and local governments and the private sector to accomplish this objective. Federal departments and agencies are directed to protect information associated with carrying out this directive. Voluntarily provided information and information that would facilitate terrorist targeting of CIKR must be handled in a manner consistent with the Homeland Security Act of 2002 and other applicable legal authorities.

Federal Information Security Management Act of 2002 (FISMA); E-Authentication Guidance for Federal Agencies, Office of Management and Budget (OMB) (December 16, 2003); FIPS Publication 199, Standards for Security Categorization of Federal Information and Information Systems (February 10, 2004); National Information Assurance Acquisition Policy for National Security Systems (NSTISSP 11); Federal Preparedness Circular 65, Federal Executive Branch Continuity of Operations (June 2004)

DOE, like other Federal agencies, is responsible for complying with FISMA as well as guidelines and practices developed by OMB that implement the law. While FISMA applies strictly to Federal Government agencies, DOE has carefully implemented requirements that support protection of the energy infrastructure. These include, for example, OMB's e-authentication guidance for remote authentication, National Institute of Standards and Technology guidelines for securing and procuring national security systems, and other related guidance.

Protected Critical Infrastructure Information (PCII) Program of the Critical Infrastructure Information Act of 2002, 6 U.S.C. §§ 131-134

The PCII Program, established pursuant to the CII Act, creates a framework that enables members of the private sector to voluntarily submit sensitive information regarding the Nation's critical infrastructure to DHS with assurance that the information, if it satisfies the requirements of the CII Act, will be protected from public disclosure. To implement and manage the program, DHS has created the PCII Program Office within DHS' Office of Infrastructure Protection. The PCII Program Office or other Federal agencies designated by the PCII program manager can receive critical infrastructure information to be validated as PCII if such information qualifies for protection under the CII Act. On September 1, 2006, DHS issued the Final Rule on Procedures for Handling Critical Infrastructure Information.

Chemical Facility Anti-Terrorism Standards (CFATS), 6 C.F.R. Part 27

In section 550 of the Department of Homeland Security Appropriations Act of 2007, Public Law 109-295, Congress gave DHS the authority to require high-risk chemical facilities to complete vulnerability assessments, develop site security plans, and implement protective measures necessary to meet DHS-defined performance standards. In accordance with this authority, on April 2, 2007, DHS released CFATS as an interim final rule.

Through CFATS, DHS established risk-based performance standards for the security of the Nation's chemical facilities. CFATS requires covered chemical facilities to prepare Security Vulnerability Assessments (SVAs), which identify facility security vulnerabilities, and to develop and implement Site Security Plans, which include measures that satisfy the identified risk-based performance standards. It also allows certain covered chemical facilities, in specified circumstances, to submit Alternate Security Programs (ASPs) in lieu of SVAs, Site Security Plans, or both.

CFATS also contains associated provisions addressing inspections and audits, recordkeeping, and protection of information that constitutes Chemical-terrorism Vulnerability Information (CVI). Finally, the rule provides DHS with authority to seek compliance through the issuance of Orders, including Orders Assessing Civil Penalty and Orders for the Cessation of Operations.

Bonneville Project Act of 1937, 16 U.S.C. § 832 et seq.; Reclamation Act of 1939, as amended, 43 U.S.C. § 485 et seq.; Flood Control Act of 1944, 16 U.S.C. § 825s; Colorado River Storage Act of 1956, 43 U.S.C. § 620 et seq.; Pacific Northwest Preferences Act of 1964, 16 U.S.C. § 837; Federal Columbia River Transmission System Act of 1974, 16 U.S.C. § 838; Department of Energy Organization Act, Section 302, 42 U.S.C. § 7152; Pacific Northwest Electric Planning and Conservation Act of 1980, 16 U.S.C. § 839 et seq.; and Energy and Water Development Appropriation Act of 1985, 16 U.S.C. § 837g

Under enabling legislation, DOE's PMAs have general powers to manage multiple areas of CIP. These range from protection to response and restoration, and cover generation, transmission, and related facilities. Congress provides similar authority to the Tennessee Valley Authority (TVA) to protect and reconstitute TVA generation, transmission, and related facilities.

Federal Power Act (FPA), 16 U.S.C. §§ 791a-825r; Public Utility Regulatory Policies Act (PURPA) of 1978, 16 U.S.C. § 2601 et seq.; Energy Policy Act of 1992, 42 U.S.C. § 13201

Congress provides a statutory foundation for FERC's oversight of power markets. While generation siting, intrastate transportation, and retail sales are generally regulated by State or local entities, wholesale sales and interstate transportation generally fall under Federal regulation, primarily by FERC.

One of FERC's strategic goals is to protect customers and market participants through vigilant and fair oversight of energy markets in transition. To pursue this goal, the Commission promotes a competitive market structure by fostering an understanding of energy market operations and using objective benchmarks to assess market conditions. FERC's Office of Market Oversight and Investigations is charged with assessing the competitive performance and efficiency of U.S. wholesale natural gas and electricity markets.

Federal Power Act, as amended, Section 202(a), 16 U.S.C. § 824a; and the Public Utility Regulatory Policies Act, Section 209(b), 16 U.S.C. §§ 824a-2

The Secretary of Energy has authority with regard to reliability of the interstate electric power transmission system. FERC has authority to define reliability regions and encourage interconnection and coordination within and between regions. DOE also has authority to gather information regarding reliability issues and make recommendations regarding industry security and reliability standards.

Defense Production Act (DPA) of 1950, as amended, Sections 101(a), 101(c), and 708, 50 U.S.C. §§ 2071 (a), (c), 2158

The Secretaries of Energy and Commerce have been delegated the President's authorities under sections 101(a) and 101(c) of DPA to require the priority performance of contracts or orders relating to materials (including energy sources), equipment, or services, including transportation, or to issue allocation orders, as necessary or appropriate for the national defense or to maximize domestic energy supplies. DPA section 101(a) permits the priority performance of contracts or orders necessary or appropriate to promote the national defense. "National defense" is defined in DPA section 702(13) to include "emergency preparedness activities conducted pursuant to title VI of the Robert T. Stafford Disaster Relief and Emergency Act and critical infrastructure protection and assurance." The Secretary of Energy has been delegated (Executive Orders 12919 and 11790) DPA section 101(a) authority with respect to all forms of energy. The Secretary of Commerce has been delegated (Executive Order 12919) the section 101(a) authority with respect to most materials, equipment, and services relevant to repair of damaged energy facilities. Section 101(c) of DPA authorizes contract priority ratings relating to contracts for materials (including energy sources), equipment, or services to maximize domestic energy supplies, if the Secretaries of Commerce and Energy, exercising their authorities delegated by Executive Order 12919, make certain findings with respect to the need for the material, equipment, or services for the exploration, production, refining, transportation, or conservation of energy supplies.

The DPA priority contracting and allocation authorities could be used to expedite repairs to damaged energy facilities, and for other purposes, including directing the supply or transportation of petroleum products, to maximize domestic energy supplies, meet defense energy needs, or support emergency preparedness activities. In the case of both the section 101(a) and 101(c) authorities, if there are contracts in place between the entity requiring priority contracting assistance and one or more suppliers of the needed good or service, DOE (with respect to the section 101(c) authority) or DOC (with respect to the section 101(a) authority) would issue an order requiring suppliers to perform under the contract on a priority basis before performing other non-rated commercial contracts. If no contracts are in place, DOE or DOC would issue a directive authorizing an entity requiring the priority contracting assistance to place a rated order with a supplier able to provide the needed materials, equipment, or services. That contractor would be required to accept the order and place it ahead of other nonrated commercial orders.

DPA section 708 provides a limited antitrust defense for industry participating in voluntary agreements "to help provide for the defense of the United States through the development of preparedness programs and the expansion of productive capacity and supply beyond levels needed to meet essential civilian demand in the United States." In the event of widespread damage to energy production or delivery systems, this authority, for example, could be used to establish a voluntary agreement of service companies to coordinate the planning of the restoration of the facilities.

Robert T. Stafford Disaster Relief and Emergency Assistance Act, as amended, 42 U.S.C. 5121 et seq.

FEMA, following a presidential declaration of emergency or major disaster, provides assistance and may require other Federal agencies to provide resources and personnel to support State and local emergency and disaster assistance efforts. Requests for a presidential declaration of emergency or major disaster must be made by the Governor of the affected State based on a finding by the Governor that the situation is of such severity and magnitude that effective response is beyond the capabilities of the State. DOE supports DHS/FEMA relief efforts by assisting Federal, State, and local governments as well as industry with their efforts to restore energy systems in disaster areas. When necessary, DOE also may deploy response staff to disaster sites. DOE is the lead agency directing ESF-12 (Energy), which assists the restoration of energy systems and provides an initial point-of-contact for the activation and deployment of DOE resources. These activities are performed pursuant to the Stafford Act, HSPD-5 (Management of Domestic Incidents) and NRF.

Chapter 24 of the Merchant Marine Act of 1920, as amended ("Jones Act"), 46 U.S.C. App. § 883

Chapter 24 of the Jones Act directs the Secretary of Homeland Security to waive the provisions requiring the use of U.S.-flag, U.S.-built, and U.S.-crewed vessels in coastwise trade, upon the request of the Secretary of Defense to the extent the Secretary of Defense deems necessary in the interest of the national defense. The act authorizes the Secretary of Homeland Security to waive compliance with the act either upon his own initiative or upon the written recommendation of the head of another agency whenever the Secretary determines that waiver is necessary in the interest of the national defense. In the case of a SPR drawdown, the President may direct the Secretary of Homeland Security to waive the Jones Act, if the volume of crude oil to be moved is significantly greater than the capacity of the existing, available U.S.-flag "Jones Act" crude oil tanker fleet. Interagency procedures have been established to expedite actions on Jones Act waiver requests during a petroleum supply disruption.

Ports and Waterways Safety Act, 33 U.S.C. § 1221 et seq., Natural Gas Pipeline Safety Act and Hazardous Liquids Pipeline Safety Act, as amended, 49 U.S.C. § 60109 et seq.

The Ports and Waterways Safety Act authorizes the Secretary of Transportation to establish vessel traffic systems for ports, harbors, and other navigable waters and control vessel traffic in areas determined to be hazardous (e.g., because of reduced visibility, adverse weather, vessel congestion, etc.) (33 U.S.C. § 1223).

Two statutes provide the framework for the Federal pipeline safety program. The Natural Gas Pipeline Safety Act of 1968 as amended authorizes DOT to regulate pipeline transportation of natural (flammable, toxic, or corrosive) gas and other gases as well as the transportation and storage of LNG. Similarly, the Hazardous Liquid Pipeline Safety Act of 1979 as amended authorizes DOT to regulate pipeline transportation of hazardous liquids (crude oil, petroleum products, anhydrous ammonia, and carbon dioxide). Both acts have been recodified as 49 U.S.C. Chapter 601. The Federal pipeline safety regulations (1) ensure safety in design, construction, inspection, testing, operation, and maintenance of pipeline facilities in the siting, construction, operation, and maintenance of LNG facilities; (2) set parameters for administering the pipeline safety program; and (3) delineate requirements for onshore oil pipeline response plans. The regulations are written as minimum performance standards.

The Magnuson Act (50 U.S.C. 191 et seq.) directs the Secretary of Transportation to issue regulations governing the movement of any vessel within U.S. territorial waters, upon a presidential declaration of a national emergency by reasons of actual or threatened war, insurrection or invasion, or disturbance or threatened disturbance of the international relations of the United States.

Maritime Transportation Security Act (MTSA), Public Law 107-295, 46 U.S.C. § 2101 et seq.

MTSA, which amended the Merchant Marine Act of 1936, requires implementation of regulations for improving the security of ports, waterfront facilities, and vessels, including those involved with the oil and gas sectors. Most energy sites with waterfront facilities are affected by MTSA and must conduct vulnerability assessments and develop security plans to be approved by the USCG.

Communications Act of 1934, as amended, 47 U.S.C. § 151 et seq., and Executive Order 12472, as amended

The National Security Emergency Preparedness Telecommunications Service Priority System, created by the National Communications System (NCS), an interagency body established by Executive Order 12472, authorizes priority treatment for restoration and provisioning (installation of new service) of certain domestic telecommunication services during several categories of emergency. Under this program, DOE is authorized to sponsor energy industry requests for priority restoration of existing telecommunications or requests for priority installation of new telecommunications as well as priority access to the Public Switch Network. Authority to order priority restoration of electric service resides in the States rather than the Federal Government. DOE, in its role supporting FEMA and DHS under the NRF as ESF-12, has been successful in requesting and obtaining priority restoration of electric service for specific important electric loads and areas.

Aviation and Transportation Security Act (ATSA), Public Law 107-71, 115 Stat. 597, November 19, 2001

As established by ATSA, TSA is responsible for security in all modes of transportation. The six modes of transportation include mass transit, aviation, maritime, highway, rail, and pipeline systems. As further noted in the NIPP, TSA is the SSA for all modes of transportation except maritime, for which the USCG is the SSA.

Critical Energy Infrastructure Information, FERC Orders 630 and 630A

FERC issued a final rule restricting access to Critical Energy Infrastructure Information and establishing new procedures for requesting access to it.

A4.2 Authorities Affecting Electric Power

Energy Policy Act of 2005, Public Law 109-58, Title XII: Electricity, Subtitle A: Reliability Standards, Section 1211: Electric Reliability Standards; Electricity Modernization Act of 2005, August 8, 2005, 42 U.S.C. § 15801; 16 U.S.C. § 824o

This subtitle provides for Federal jurisdiction over certain activities that are required to support reliability of the U.S. bulk power system. Title XII authorizes FERC to certify a national Electric Reliability Organization (ERO) to enforce mandatory reliability standards for the bulk-power system. FERC will oversee the ERO in the United States and all ERO standards must be approved by FERC. The ERO can impose penalties on a user, owner, or operator of the bulk-power system for violations of any FERC-approved reliability standard, but such penalties are subject to FERC review and potential change.

FERC Order Issued in Docket No. RR06-1-000, Certifying NERC as the Electric Reliability Organization, July 20, 2006

Pursuant to EPAct of 2005, FERC conditionally certified NERC as the Nation's ERO. NERC must make specified changes and file them with FERC in order to continue as the ERO. As the ERO, NERC will be responsible for developing and enforcing mandatory electric reliability standards under FERC's oversight. The standards will apply to all users, owners, and operators of the bulk-power system.

FERC Order 706 Issued in Docket No. RM06-22-000, Mandatory Reliability Standards for Critical Infrastructure Protection, January 18, 2008

Pursuant to section 215 of FPA, FERC approved eight CIP Reliability Standards submitted to FERC for approval by NERC. The standards require certain users, owners, and operators of the bulk power system to comply with specific requirements to safeguard critical cyber assets.

FERC Order Issued in Docket No. RD09-7-000, Approving Revised Reliability Standards for Critical Infrastructure Protection and Requiring Compliance Filing, September 30, 2009

Pursuant to section 215(d)(5) of the FPA, FERC in Order 706 directed NERC to develop modifications to the eight CIP Reliability Standards using its Reliability Standards Development Process. On May 22, 2009, NERC filed revised Reliability Standards for Critical Infrastructure Protection. In its filing, NERC indicated it is developing responsive modifications in multiple phases, and the instant filing represents the results of the first phase of the initiative. The revised CIP Reliability Standards will become effective April 1, 2010.

Federal Power Act, 16 U.S.C. §§ 791a-825r; Public Utility Regulatory Policies Act, 16 U.S.C. § 2705; DOE Organization Act, 42 U.S.C. §§ 7101-7352; 18 C.F.R. Parts 4, 12, and 16; MOU between FERC, Army Corps of Engineers and Bureau of Reclamation

Congress authorizes FERC to oversee the Nation's non-Federal hydropower infrastructure. Congressional and other legal delegations also define hydropower responsibilities among FERC and other agencies, such as USACE and BOR.

With regard to FERC authorities, delegations in the FPA include a range of activities, such as issuing licenses for non-Federal hydropower projects; requiring safety and operating conditions; investigating and taking over facilities (or levying fines) for administrative violations, such as safety and security; defining construction, maintenance, and operation requirements by licensees; and other acts to carry out the purposes of the FPA. In addition, section 405(d) of PURPA, 16 U.S.C. § 2705, authorizes a hydropower project's exemption from licensing under certain conditions. Finally, the Department of Energy Organization Act, 42 U.S.C. §§ 7101-7352: Title IV establishes FERC (as the successor agency to the Federal Power Commission) and enumerates its authority regarding hydropower facilities.

In addition to congressional delegations, regulations further define FERC authorities over hydropower facilities. These rules address such issues as project safety and security, procedures for relicensing or Federal takeover of licensed hydropower projects, and investigations.

FERC has several MOUs with regard to hydropower facilities:

- **USACE**, which has responsibility for ownership and operation of Federal dams for electric power production and other purposes. This MOU describes procedures for agency cooperation during the processing of hydropower applications to facilitate the investigation, construction, operation, and maintenance of FERC-licensed hydro projects at USACE dams.

- **BOR**, which has responsibility for ownership and operation of dams for electric power production and other purposes. This MOU describes procedures for agency cooperation during the processing of hydropower applications to facilitate the investigation, construction, operation, and maintenance of FERC-licensed hydro projects at BOR dams.

Executive Order 10485, Providing for the Performance of Certain Functions Heretofore Performed by the President with Respect to Electric Power and Natural Gas Facilities Located on the Borders of the United States, September 3, 1953, as amended by Executive Order 12038, Relating to Certain Functions Transferred to the Secretary of Energy by the Department of Energy Organization Act, February 3, 1978

DOE is authorized to issue presidential permits for the construction, operation, maintenance, and connection of electric transmission facilities at U.S. international borders if it determines that the issuance of such a permit is in the public interest. In determining whether issuance of the permit is consistent with the public interest, DOE considers the impact the proposed project would have on the operating reliability of the U.S. electric power supply and the environmental impacts of the proposed project pursuant to the National Environmental Policy Act (NEPA) of 1969, and any other factors that DOE may also consider relevant to the public interest. DOE must also obtain favorable recommendations from the Secretary of State and Secretary of Defense before issuing a permit.

Federal Power Act, as amended, Section 202(c), 16 U.S.C. § 824a(c)

The Secretary of Energy has authority in time of war or other emergency to order temporary interconnections of facilities and generation, delivery, interchange, or transmission of electric energy that the Secretary deems necessary to meet an emergency. This authority may be used upon receipt of a petition from a party requesting the emergency action or it may be initiated by DOE on its own initiative.

Federal Power Act, as amended, § 202(e), 16 U.S.C. § 824a(e)

Exports of electricity from the United States to a foreign country are regulated by FERC pursuant to sections 301(b) and 402(f) of the Department of Energy Organization Act (42 U.S.C. 7151(b), 7172(f)) and require authorization under section 202(e) of FPA (16 U.S.C. § 824a(e)).

Department of Energy Organization Act and FPA, 10 CFR Parts 205.350-205.353

DOE has authority to obtain current information regarding emergency situations in the electric supply systems in the United States. DOE has established mandatory reporting requirements for electric power system incidents or possible incidents. This reporting is required to meet DOE's national security requirements and other responsibilities contained in NRF.

Power Plant and Industrial Fuel Use Act (FUA), § 404(a), 42 U.S.C. § 8374(a)

Under section 404(a), the President has authority to allocate coal (and require the transportation of coal) for use by any power plant or major fuel-burning installation during a declared severe energy supply interruption as defined by section 3(8) of EPCA, 42 U.S.C. § 6202(8). The President may also exercise such allocation authority upon a published finding that a national or regional fuel supply shortage exists or may exist that the President determines is, or is likely to be, of significant scope and duration, and of an emergency nature; causes, or may cause, major adverse impact on public health, safety, welfare or on the economy; and results, or is likely to result, from an interruption in the supply of coal or from sabotage, or from an act of God. Section 404(e) stipulates that the President may not delegate his authority to issue orders under this authority. It does not, however, prevent the President from directing any Federal agency to issue rules or regulations, or take other action consistent with section 404, in the implementation of such an order.

The FUA section 404(a) authority could be used to help provide coal as an alternative fuel source to electric power plants and other major fuel-burning installations that have received orders prohibiting the burning of natural gas or petroleum as a primary energy source, assuming these facilities actually have the capability to burn coal. Many likely do not, so the authority may be of limited utility. This authority also could be used during a coal supply shortage to ensure that coal-burning electric power plants or major fuel-burning installations have adequate supplies of coal.

As an alternative to the use of FUA section 404(a), the President, or the President's delegate(s), could allocate coal supplies under the authority of section 101(a) of DPA, 50 U.S.C. App. § 2071(a) and Executive Order 12919 (1994).

Clean Air Act, 42 U.S.C. § 7401 et seq.

Section 110(f) of the Clean Air Act permits a State Governor to issue an emergency temporary suspension of any part of a State Implementation Plan (SIP) (as well as a temporary waiver of penalties for excess SOx or NOx emissions) in accordance with the following: (1) the owner/operator of a fuel-burning source petitions the State for relief; (2) the Governor gives notice and opportunity for public hearing on the petition; (3) the Governor finds that an emergency exists in the vicinity of the source involving high levels of unemployment or loss of necessary energy supplies for residential dwellings, and that the unemployment or loss can be totally or partially alleviated by an emergency suspension of SIP requirements applicable to the petitioning source; (4) the President, in response to the Governor's request, declares a national or regional emergency exists of such severity that a temporary SIP suspension may be necessary and other means of responding to the energy emergency may be inadequate; and (5) the Governor issues an emergency suspension to the source. DOE may be asked to advise the President of fuel supply situations regarding requests for presidential emergency declarations for SIP relief.

A4.3 Authorities Affecting Natural Gas

Natural Gas Act, Sections 3 and 7, 15 U.S.C. § 717 et seq.

DOE has authority under section 3 to issue orders, upon application, to authorize imports and exports of natural gas. Section 3 requires DOE to approve, without modification or delay, applications to import LNG and applications to import and export natural gas from and to countries with which there is a free-trade agreement in effect requiring national treatment for trade in natural gas. Section 7 provides FERC the authority to approve the siting of and abandonment of interstate natural gas facilities, including pipelines, storage, and LNG facilities. Under the Natural Gas Act FERC has the authority to review and evaluate certificate applications for facilities to transport, exchange, or store natural gas; acquire, construct, and operate facilities for such service; and to extend or abandon such facilities. In this context, FERC approvals include the siting of said facilities and the evaluation of alternative locations. FERC jurisdiction does not include production, gathering, or distribution facilities, or those strictly for intrastate service. In reference to regulating imports and exports of natural gas under section 3 of the Natural Gas Act, Executive Order 10485, as amended by Executive Order 12038, and sections 301(b), 402(e), and (f) of the Department of Energy Organization Act (42 U.S.C. § 7101 et seq.), the Secretary has delegated to FERC authority over the construction, operation, and siting of particular facilities. With respect to natural gas, that authority covers the construction of new domestic facilities, the place of entry for imports, and the place of exit for exports. FERC also has authority to approve or deny an application for the siting, construction, expansion, and operation of an LNG terminal under section 3 of the Natural Gas Act.

Natural Gas Policy Act, Title III, Sections 301-303, 15 U.S.C. § 717 et seq.

DOE may order any interstate pipeline or local distribution company served by an interstate pipeline to allocate natural gas in order to assist in meeting the needs of high-priority consumers during a natural gas emergency. DOE has delegated authority (Executive Order 12235) under sections 302 and 303, respectively, of the Natural Gas Policy Act, to authorize purchases of natural gas and to allocate supplies of natural gas in interstate commerce to assist in meeting natural gas requirements for high-priority uses, upon a finding by the President under section 301 of an existing or imminent natural gas supply emergency (15 U.S.C. §§ 3361-3363). The declaration of a natural gas supply emergency is the legal precondition for the emergency purchase and allocation authority in sections 302 and 303, respectively, of the Natural Gas Policy Act.

Although Executive Order 12235 delegates to the Secretary of Energy the emergency purchase and allocation authorities in sections 302 and 303, respectively, the President has not delegated his authority to declare a natural gas supply emergency. Nothing in the Natural Gas Policy Act would preclude such a presidential delegation.

Under section 301 of the Natural Gas Policy Act, the President may declare a natural gas supply emergency if he makes certain findings. The President must find that a severe natural gas shortage, endangering the supply of natural gas for high-priority uses, exists or is imminent in the United States or in any region of the country. Further, the President must find that the exercise of the emergency natural gas purchase authority under section 302 of the Natural Gas Policy Act, of the emergency allocation authority under section 303 of the Natural Gas Policy Act, or of the emergency conversion authority of section 607 of PURPA is reasonably necessary, having exhausted other alternatives to the maximum extent practicable, to assist in meeting natural gas requirements for high-priority uses. The emergency terminates on the date the President finds that a shortage either no longer exists or is not imminent, or 120 days after the date of the emergency declaration, whichever is earlier.

Public Utility Regulatory Policies Act of 1978, Section 607, 15 U.S.C. § 717z, and Section 404(b) of the Power Plant and Industrial Fuel Use Act, 42 U.S.C. § 8374(b)

There are two authorities that can be used in emergency situations to require utilities to switch from natural gas and petroleum for electric power generation. DOE has delegated authority (Executive Order 12235) under section 607(a) of PURPA, following the President's finding of a natural gas supply emergency, to prohibit the burning of natural gas by any electric power plant or major fuel-burning installation. The required emergency finding is identical to that in the Natural Gas Policy Act (15 U.S.C. § 717z). As explained in the previous section discussing the Natural Gas Policy Act, under section 301 of the Natural Gas Policy Act and 607(a) of PURPA, the President may declare a natural gas supply emergency if he makes certain findings. The President must find that a severe natural gas shortage, endangering the supply of natural gas for high-priority uses, exists or is imminent in the United States. The PURPA fuel-switching authority is similar to the presidential authority contained in section 404(b) of FUA, 42 U.S.C 8374(b), to prohibit the burning of natural gas or petroleum by electric power plants or major fuel-burning installations.

Section 404(b) of FUA provides that the President may by order prohibit the use by any power plant or major fuel-burning installation of petroleum or natural gas, or both, as a primary energy source. A legal precondition to such a presidential order is the President's finding of a severe energy supply interruption, as defined by section 3(8) of EPCA, 42 U.S.C. § 6202(8). Section 404(e) stipulates that the President may not delegate his authority to issue orders under this authority. It does not, however, prevent the President from directing any Federal agency to issue rules or regulations, or take other action consistent with section 404, in the implementation of such order.

Emergency Reconstruction, FERC Order 633

Amended FERC regulations enable interstate natural gas pipeline companies, under emergency conditions, to replace mainline facilities using—if necessary—a route other than the existing right-of-way, and to waive the 45-day prior notice requirement and cost constraints. This order comes into effect when immediate action is needed to restore service in an emergency caused by a sudden unanticipated loss of natural gas or capacity, and when restoration is needed to prevent loss of life, impairment of health, or damage to property. In such emergencies, the amended regulations allow pipeline companies to proceed with construction before the end of the separate 30-day prior notice period to landowners, if all necessary easements have been obtained. This initiative was implemented in the wake of the events of September 11, 2001, to help ensure the security of the natural gas pipeline infrastructure without compromising FERC's responsibilities under NEPA.

A4.4 Authorities Affecting Petroleum

Energy Policy and Conservation Act, Sections 151-180, 42 U.S.C. §§ 6231-6251

Sections 151-191 of EPCA authorize DOE to establish and operate the SPR. Section 161(d)(1) authorizes the President to order drawdown and sale of products from the SPR upon a finding that drawdown is required either by a "severe energy supply interruption" or obligations of the United States under the Agreement on an International Energy Program (IEP)(42 U.S.C. § 6241(d)(1)).

Section 161(h) empowers the President to drawdown the SPR in circumstances other than a "severe energy supply interruption" or a need to meet U.S. obligations under IEP, if: (1) the President finds that a circumstance "exists that constitutes, or is likely to become, a domestic or international energy supply shortage of significant scope and duration"; (2) the President determines that drawdown "would assist directly or significantly in preventing or reducing the adverse impact of such a shortage"; and (3) the Secretary of Defense has found that the action taken will not impair national security. However, there are several limitations on the use of this authority: The reserve may not be drawn down for more than 30 million barrels or for longer than 60 days with respect to a single event. Furthermore, drawdowns under this authority may not reduce the reserve to a level below 500 million barrels (42. U.S.C. § 6241(h)). EPCA gives the President authority to allow the export of crude oil withdrawn from the SPR during a drawdown for refining or exchange outside the United States in connection with an arrangement for the delivery of refined petroleum products to the United States (42. U.S.C. § 6241(i)). In recognition of this authority, DOC has provided for automatic approval for export of SPR oil for these purposes in its Export Administration Regulations at 15 CFR Part 754.

Energy Policy and Conservation Act, Sections 181-184, 42 U.S.C. §§ 6250-6250c

Pursuant to section 181 of EPCA, 42 U.S.C. § 6250, the Secretary establishes and maintains a home heating oil reserve of 2 million barrels in the Northeast. This reserve is not part of the SPR. The Secretary may sell products from the Northeast Home Oil Reserve following a presidential finding that there is a "severe energy supply interruption" in accordance with EPCA section 183(a). This finding would specify that a dislocation in the heating oil market has resulted from the interruption, or from the existence of a regional supply shortage of significant size and duration, and that action under this section would assist directly and significantly in reducing the shortage's adverse impacts.

Section 363 of the Energy Policy and Conservation Act, 42 U.S.C. § 6322(e)

To be eligible for financial assistance to assist in development and implementation of an energy conservation plan, a State must submit to the Secretary of Energy, as a supplement to its energy conservation plan, an energy emergency planning program for an energy supply disruption as designated by the State consistent with applicable Federal and State law. The contingency plan, "shall include an implementation strategy or strategies (including regional coordination) for dealing with energy emergencies."

Appendix 5: Asset Ownership

Major energy asset ownership includes the following entities:

- **Federal Government**. The Federal Government is a major owner of energy assets and critical infrastructure throughout the United States and its Territories. Examples include TVA, a major owner of hydroelectric dams, nuclear and fossil power generation stations, and high-voltage transmission; BOR, a major dam owner; DOE, which oversees the SPR and the Northeast Home Heating Oil Reserve; and power administrations such as the Western Area Power Administration and the Bonneville Power Administration.

- **State and local governments**. State and especially local governments own substantial energy assets. These include all municipal utilities, many of which own generation and electric and/or natural gas distribution systems, and are primarily self-regulated.

- **Regulated utilities**. Regulated utilities own most of the electric and natural gas infrastructure in the United States, and although they are private sector entities, most are rate-regulated at the Federal, State, and/or local levels. Included in this category are major interstate pipeline companies, hydroelectric facilities, storage facility operators, and LNG terminal owners, all of which are regulated by FERC.

- **Unregulated energy companies**.[62] Unregulated energy companies are those whose rates are not directly regulated by FERC or a State public utility commission, and therefore charge market-based rates for the power they produce. Many of these companies own energy infrastructure assets, such as merchant generation companies owning power plants that participate in wholesale power markets. Unregulated marketing and trading companies are also active in acquiring, storing, and trading natural gas, crude oil, electricity, and petroleum products.

- **Unregulated non-energy companies**. Unregulated, non-energy, private sector companies, like those in the chemical, aluminum, forest products, and telecommunications industries, own energy assets including generation plants, refineries, and oil and gas production facilities.

- **Cooperatives**. Significant energy infrastructure is owned by cooperatives, especially in the electric distribution sector. These assets, which can include generation, transmission, and distribution, are generally "nonjurisdictional," meaning their rates are not regulated by FERC or the States.

- **Foreign entities**. Some U.S. energy infrastructure is owned by foreign energy concerns, including several utilities, power stations, and other asset classes. Many U.S. energy companies also own energy infrastructure in foreign countries. These U.S.-owned foreign assets may or may not be directly related to meeting energy supply needs in the United States.

---

62 EPAct of 2005 mandated that FERC establish an ERO with powers to enforce rules affecting the reliability of the Nation's electric grid. NERC has been designated by FERC as the ERO. All users of the Nation's high-voltage electric grid will be subject to these mandatory reliability rules, even if they are not otherwise regulated by FERC for rates or tariffs.

Appendix 6: Energy SCC and GCC Membership

Members of the Electricity Sector Coordinating Council
Allegheny Power
American Public Power Association
Arizona Public Service
Arkansas Electric Cooperative Corporation
Dominion Resources
Edison Electric Institute
Electric Power Supplier Association
Exelon Corporation
Hydro One, Ontario, Canada
Independent Electricity System Operator, Ontario, Canada
ISO/RTO Council
National Rural Electric Cooperative Association
New York Independent System Operator
North American Electric Reliability Corporation
Reliability First Corporation
Southern Company

Members of the Oil and Natural Gas Sector Coordinating Council
AGL Resources, Inc.
American Exploration and Production Council
American Gas Association
American Petroleum Institute
American Public Gas Association
Anadarko Canada Corporation
Association of Oil Pipe Lines
Canadian Association of Petroleum Producers
Canadian Energy Pipeline Association
Center for Liquefied Natural Gas
Chevron Corporation
Colonial Pipeline Company
ConocoPhillips Company
Dominion Resources, Inc.
Duke Energy Corporation
Edison Chouest Offshore, LLC
El Paso Corporation
Enbridge, Inc.
Energy Security Council
ExxonMobil
Flint Hills Resources, LP
Gas Processors Association
Genesis Energy, Inc.
Independent Liquid Terminals Association
Independent Petroleum Association of America

International Association of Drilling Contractors

Interstate Natural Gas Association of America

Kinder Morgan Energy Partners, LP

Leffler Energy

Marathon Petroleum Company, LLC

MSW Consulting, LLC

National Association of Convenience Stores

National Ocean Industries Association

National Petrochemical and Refiners Association

National Propane Gas Association

NiSource Inc.

Noble Drilling Services Inc.

Offshore Marine Service Association

Offshore Operators Committee

Petroleum Fuel and Terminal Company

Petroleum Marketers Association of America

Questar Gas Company

Rowan Companies, Inc.

Sempra Energy

Shell Oil Company

Shipley Stores, LLC

Society of Independent Gasoline Marketers of America

Spectra Energy

Suncor Energy, Inc.

U.S. Oil and Gas Association

Valero Energy Corporation

Western States Petroleum Association

Williams Energy Services, LLC

Participants in the Energy Government Coordinating Council
United States Army Corps of Engineers
United States Department of Agriculture, Rural Utilities Service
United States Department of Defense
United States Department of Energy, Office of Electricity Delivery and Energy Reliability
United States Department of Energy, Office of Fossil Energy
United States Department of Health and Human Services
United States Department of Homeland Security, Office of Infrastructure Protection
United States Department of Homeland Security, Transportation Security Administration
United States Department of Homeland Security, United States Coast Guard
United States Department of the Interior, Minerals Management Service
United States Department of State, International Boundary and Water Commission
United States Department of Transportation, Committee on the Marine Transportation System
United States Department of Transportation, Maritime Administration
United States Department of Transportation, Pipeline and Hazardous Materials Safety Administration
United States Department of the Treasury
United States Environmental Protection Agency
Canadian Department of Natural Resources
Federal Energy Regulatory Commission
National Association of Regulatory Utility Commissioners
National Association of State Energy Officials
National Governors Association
Transportation Security Administration's Pipeline Security Division

Appendix 7: Transportation Systems SSP: Pipeline Executive Summary

Each day, thousands of businesses and millions of people rely on the safe, secure, and efficient movement of commodities through the transportation system. Manmade or natural disruptions to this critical system could result in significant harm to the social and economic well-being of the country. The Nation's pipeline system is a mode of transportation with unique infrastructure security characteristics and requirements.

As stipulated in the Transportation Systems SSP, (TSPP) the Pipeline Modal Implementation Plan was developed to ensure the security and resilience of the pipeline sector. The vision of this plan is to ensure that the pipeline sector is secure, resilient, and able to quickly detect physical and cyber intrusion or attack, mitigate the adverse consequences of an incident, and quickly restore pipeline service. A robust, nationwide pipeline security program will instill public confidence in the reliability of the Nation's critical energy infrastructure, enhance public safety, and ensure the continued functioning of other critical infrastructure sectors that depend on secure and reliable supplies of products for consumption.

The TSSP Base Plan and the Pipeline Modal Implementation Plan were developed, reviewed, and updated using both the Transportation Systems Sector and the Energy Sector GCC and SCC frameworks. In accordance with NIPP, a CIPAC Oil and Natural Gas (ONG) Joint Sector Committee was established to provide a legal framework for members of the Energy Sector GCC and ONG SCC to engage in joint CIP discussions and activities, including those involved with pipeline security. Under this CIPAC committee, a Pipeline Working Group writing team was formed to develop and review applicable SSPs, including the Energy SSP and the TSSP. The writing team reviewed and commented on the draft TSSP Base Plan and drafted the Pipeline Modal Implementation Plan. The draft plans were distributed to the pipeline industry via the GCC and SCC memberships for another level of review and input before finalizing the documents.

TSA Pipeline Security will work with its security partners in both the Transportation and Energy sectors to update the TSSP Base Plan and Pipeline Modal Implementation Plan regularly, as called for in the NIPP. Any changes will be developed and shared with pipeline partners collaboratively through the GCC/SCC/CIPAC framework.

The core of the plan is a pipeline system relative risk assessment and prioritization methodology. This methodology provides a logical prioritization process to systematically list, analyze, and sort pipeline systems and critical pipeline components within those pipeline systems. By prioritization, security resources can be effectively used to manage risk mitigation in order to protect critical pipelines from terrorist threats. The methodology is based on the Transportation Sector Systems-Based Risk Management (SBRM) methodology, which is in turn based on the risk management framework presented in the NIPP.

With a view toward this end state, the TSSP Base Plan and this Pipeline Modal Implementation Plan specifically focus on how the Transportation Sector will continue to enhance the security of its CIKR. Programs to protect the Nation's pipeline systems are key to making the Nation safer, more secure, and more resilient in the face of terrorist attacks and other hazards.

Appendix 8: Asset Classes

This appendix provides greater detail on asset classes and information parameters for the electricity, petroleum, and natural gas sectors. Major asset categories are shown in chapter 1, table 1-1, which provides categorization and clear distinction of energy infrastructure asset types that allow public and private sector partners to properly plan for energy infrastructure protection. Some energy asset categories are the responsibility of agencies other than DOE. For example, DHS, working with the Nuclear Regulatory Commission, is responsible for commercial nuclear power plants; DHS is responsible for dams; and working with DOT, DHS/TSA also has responsibility for oil and gas pipelines. These key components of the energy infrastructure will be closely coordinated with the responsible sector teams. For example, the members of the ONG SCC also work on transportation pipeline efforts.

Many existing sources of energy attribute data can be used for energy infrastructure protection planning and analysis. Major sources are described in the table below.

Table A8-1: Sources of Existing Energy Asset Data

Category	Entity	Comments
Federal Government	Department of Energy/Office of Fossil Energy	Statistical data on natural gas pipeline imports and exports from Canada and Mexico, as well as LNG imports and exports. Most data relate to quantities, volumes, prices, and shippers.
	Department of Homeland Security/ Transportation Security Administration	Data related to pipeline security.
	Department of Homeland Security/ United States Coast Guard	Data on port safety and security activities; data on indicators and warnings of threats and communications.
	Department of the Interior/ Bureau of Reclamation	Data on federally owned dams.
	Department of the Interior/ Minerals Management Service	Data on offshore oil and gas.
	Department of Transportation/ Pipeline and Hazardous Materials Safety Administration	Data related to pipeline safety.
	Energy Information Administration	Statistical energy data on a variety of electric, oil, and gas variables. Most data relate to quantities (volumes, throughputs) and prices.
	Federal Energy Regulatory Commission	Data on electric transmission, generation, hydropower, and interstate pipelines for regulatory and cost-of-service purposes.
	Environmental Protection Agency	Data on generation plants and refineries relative to environmental compliance.
	United States Department of Agriculture/ Rural Utilities Service	Monitors/regulates 65 generation and transmission co-ops.
State Governments	National Conference of State Legislatures	Variety of data related to legislative decision making.
	Public Utility Commissions; National Association of Regulatory Utility Commissioners	Data on electric and gas generation, transmission, and distribution for regulatory, cost-of-service, and emergency purposes.
	State Energy Offices / Commissions / R&D Authorities / Homeland Security	Data on in-State assets, supply and demand, and R&D; information on State-level programs. Examples include California Energy Commission and New York State Energy Research and Development Authority.
	State Environmental Offices	Data related to energy asset environmental compliance.

Category	Entity	Comments
Nongovernmental Organizations	American Gas Association	Gas utility data.
	American Petroleum Institute	Petroleum industry data.
	American Public Power Association	Public power (municipal) data.
	Edison Electric Institute	Electric utility data.
	Electric Power Research Institute; Electricity Innovation Institute	Electric R&D data.
	Independent System Operators (e.g., CA-ISO, NY ISO, ISO-NE, PJM, MISO)	Competitive electric market data.
	Gas Technology Institute	Gas R&D data.
	National Association of State Energy Officials	Data on State energy emergency plans and variety of data regarding State Energy Office programs.
	National Petrochemical & Refiners Association	Petroleum data.
	North American Electric Reliability Corporation	National electric reliability data.
	The eight North American regional electric reliability councils (see **www. nerc.org**)	Regional electric reliability data.
Private Energy Companies	Regulated and unregulated energy companies	Data on system-specific operations and most distribution data.
Data Vendors	Platts/RDI, Penwell, etc.	Energy Sector data sold for profit.

www.ingramcontent.com/pod-product-compliance
Lightning Source LLC
Chambersburg PA
CBHW080301290526
45790CB00005B/1884